THE SHOOTING SCRIPT®

THE BURNING PLAIN

THE BURNING PLAIN

SCREENPLAY AND INTRODUCTION BY
GUILLERMO ARRIAGA

A Newmarket Shooting Script® Series Book
NEWMARKET PRESS • NEW YORK

The Newmarket Shooting Script® Series is a registered trademark of
Newmarket Publishing & Communications Company.

This book is published simultaneously in the United States of America and in Canada.

FIRST EDITION

10 9 8 7 6 5 4 3 2 1

ISBN: 978-1-55704-826-4

Library of Congress Catalog-in-Publication Data available upon request.

QUANTITY PURCHASES

Companies, professional groups, clubs, and other organizations may qualify for special terms when ordering quantities
of this title. For information e-mail sales@newmarketpress.com or write to Special Sales, Newmarket Press, 18 East
48th Street, New York, NY 10017; call (212) 832-3575 ext. 19 or 1-800-669-3903; FAX (212) 832-3629.

Website: www.newmarketpress.com

Manufactured in the United States of America.

OTHER BOOKS IN THE NEWMARKET SHOOTING SCRIPT® SERIES INCLUDE:

About a Boy: The Shooting Script
Adaptation: The Shooting Script
The Age of Innocence: The Shooting Script
American Beauty: The Shooting Script
A Beautiful Mind: The Shooting Script
The Birdcage: The Shooting Script
Black Hawk Down: The Shooting Script
Capote: The Shooting Script
The Constant Gardener: The Shooting Script
Dan in Real Life: The Shooting Script
Dead Man Walking: The Shooting Script
*Eternal Sunshine of the Spotless Mind:
    The Shooting Script*
Gods and Monsters: The Shooting Script
Gosford Park: The Shooting Script
Human Nature: The Shooting Script
Juno: The Shooting Script
Knocked Up: The Shooting Script

The Ice Storm: The Shooting Script
Little Miss Sunshine: The Shooting Script
Margot at the Wedding: The Shooting Script
Michael Clayton: The Shooting Script
Milk: The Shooting Script
The People vs. Larry Flynt: The Shooting Script
Punch-Drunk Love: The Shooting Script
The Savages: The Shooting Script
The Shawshank Redemption: The Shooting Script
Sideways: The Shooting Script
Slumdog Millionaire: The Shooting Script
The Squid and the Whale: The Shooting Script
Stranger Than Fiction: The Shooting Script
Synecdoche, New York: The Shooting Script
Taking Woodstock: The Shooting Script
Traffic: The Shooting Script
The Truman Show: The Shooting Script
War of the Worlds: The Shooting Script

OTHER NEWMARKET PICTORIAL MOVIEBOOKS AND NEWMARKET INSIDER FILM BOOKS INCLUDE:

Angels & Demons: The Illustrated Movie Companion
The Art of Monsters vs. Aliens
*The Art of X2**
The Art of X-Men: The Last Stand
*Bram Stoker's Dracula: The Film and the Legend**
*Chicago: The Movie and Lyrics**
*Dances with Wolves: The Illustrated Story of the Epic Film**
Dreamgirls
*E.T. The Extra-Terrestrial: From Concept to Classic**
Gladiator: The Making of the Ridley Scott Epic Film

*Good Night, and Good Luck: The Screenplay and History Behind
    the Landmark Movie**
*Hotel Rwanda: Bringing the True Story of an African Hero to Film**
The Jaws Log
The Mummy: Tomb of the Dragon Emperor
*Ray: A Tribute to the Movie, the Music, and the Man**
Saving Private Ryan: The Men, The Mission, The Movie
Schindler's List: Images of the Steven Spielberg Film
*Superbad: The Illustrated Moviebook**
Tim Burton's Corpse Bride: An Invitation to the Wedding

*Includes Screenplay

CONTENTS

INTRODUCTION

BY GUILLERMO ARRIAGA

Once when I was ten or eleven years old, I was playing soccer with my friends on our neighborhood street and a kid came running up, screaming, "Fire, fire." We looked up, and blocks away we could see a long column of smoke rising into the sky. We jumped on our bikes and headed toward it just as fast as we could.

A house was on fire, burning furiously. We could feel the intense heat. Huge flames shot out from the windows. Some of the neighbors gathered outside the house, shocked and scared. Someone said that some people might be trapped inside.

The scene changed quickly before my eyes. What had started as something that aroused our curiosity had become this tragic event. And there was nothing anyone could do. The fire was so powerful that it would have immediately killed anyone who tried to act like a hero.

The firemen arrived and spent several hours trying to bring the inferno under control. To ease our fears, they said it was fortunate that no one had been inside. Maybe it was just a white lie, a story made up to calm us. We never found out for sure since apparently a new family we had never met had recently moved in.

The image of someone burning alive haunted me for many years. It did so in such a profound way that I wrote two screenplays about a house on fire. The first, *A Fuego Lento* (*Slowly Roasted*), I wrote immediately after *Amores Perros,* and it hasn't been shot yet. This screenplay tells eleven stories in real time about several characters going to watch a house on fire. It is written in a dark, humorous tone. For some strange reason, someone acting in bad faith said that *Amores Perros* started as eleven stories and was later reduced to three. This falsehood was even listed on Wikipedia, but it's absolutely untrue. *Amores Perros* was always structured in three stories. Its structure is based on *The Sound and the Fury*, the masterpiece by William Faulkner, and by a car accident I suffered. The structure reflects what happened before the accident, during the accident, and after the accident.

The other screenplay that was influenced by that house on fire is this one, *The Burning Plain*. Haunted for years by the flames coming out of those windows, I wrote the first scene of the screenplay as a direct reference to that remote episode in my life.

However, a single image doesn't make a story. There were many others that I accumulated through life's experiences that have contributed to the story line. For instance, there was the trailer home in the middle of a sorghum field that was the love nest of two gay, married American men who used the excuse of hunting trips to Mexico to carry out their clandestine affair.

Another: I was driving with my hunting friends on a road contiguous to a sorghum field when suddenly, out of nowhere, a crop duster plane flying six feet above the ground started spraying just a dozen yards away from us. It was a close call, an almost imminent crash. No one had told us there was going to be a plane spraying the fields. No one had told the pilot that we were thinking of hunting that afternoon. Of course the pilot was furious at us. But after chatting for a while, things calmed down and I learned a little about the life and job of a crop-dusting pilot, a job that I don't recall having ever been portrayed in a film (maybe it has, but I don't remember it).

And then I once met a girl who had this obsessive need for sex. She didn't really care with whom. She just had this sad compulsion of basically fucking whoever she was slightly attracted to. She even boasted that she had had sex with ten guys in a night club in one night. I asked her why she kept doing it. Her answer was painfully ambiguous: "To find myself."

These stories and many others remained in my thoughts for years. But I required a concept, something that would allow them to come together as a whole. It was during a hunting trip that the idea came to me: the four elements. I was sitting beside a huge dam in the state of Tamaulipas when I began thinking of the old notion that our personality is influenced by each of the elements. Men and women of fire, of earth, of water, of air. Then these elements began to translate into visual and narrative leitmotifs.

So I decided to tell four stories, each one determined by one of the four elements. This creative choice allowed me to structure the screenplay, to understand the characters, to build the visual world of the film. In the beginning the screenplay was titled "The Four Elements."

But I also decided to represent these four elements in a very subtle way, imperceptible to the eyes of the viewers and the readers. It was the secret clue that informed the screenplay.

The first image of the film is a trailer home on fire in a vast and isolated desert plain. After it, the stories determined by the other elements begin to be told. There is the one of Sylvia, naked in a balcony before a river in a cloudy city (water). Then there are the two kids, Santiago and Cristobal, exploring the charred trailer home where their father was burned alive while making love to the married woman he was having an affair with (fire). This is followed by the crop duster pilots Carlos and older Santiago, with his daughter Maria, going to a job in a sorghum field in Mexico (air) and the last is the affair between Nick and Gina that begins on a dusty road and continues in a trailer home full of dirt (earth).

I have never repeated any of the structures that I have used before. Each script I have written has a different construction. What makes them similar are the themes. Since these have been very personal scripts, my obsessions and vital concerns repeat time and again: the weight of a death over the survivors, the search for identity, the intense consequences of our own acts, forbidden love, characters on the edge of abysses, the need for personal redemption. Without being aware of it as I was writing, it has been pointed out that I tend to use recurring images, locations, and actions. For example, the constant presence of motels and hospitals; the chance of an amputation or a mutilation; the extensive use of cars. None of these are intentional. They just appear in one way or another, like a subterranean flow of images and places I have no control over. All of this is inevitable. It happens when you write from the deepest stories accumulated through life.

The structure of *The Burning Plain* differs from the other films I have written in the sense that this is only one story, but told through different time frames. We watch the characters through a period of around twelve years. I wanted to create a story of connections and consequences. What a character does one day has repercussions another day many years later. That is why I decided to write the final montage of the doors and windows.

Also I wanted to hold back on some of the background information about the characters. I have always thought that audiences are extremely intelligent and sophisticated and that they're capable of filling in the gaps. Quite deliberately I refrained from giving too much information about the characters. For example, I never wanted the audience to know where or how Nick and Gina met. I didn't include any moments of Nick with his family. I avoided a closure between old Mariana and old Santiago at the hospital. I think that there is an inherent beauty in allowing the viewers to elaborate their own conclusions, to explain characters in their terms and not in the terms of the writer.

The screenplay went through a lot of revisions. In the beginning I wasn't attached to direct it. I just sold the pitch to Walter Parkes and Laurie McDonald, who planned on finding a director for it. I must say that both of them were crucial to this project. They were ruthless and always gave intelligent and sensible notes. In contrast to other writers, I truly enjoy notes that challenge me and make me rethink a screenplay, which is something that Walter and Laurie did beautifully, with a great deal of good taste, a strong sense of story, and a precise knowledge of character development.

Also, I have a group of friends who always read my work in progress. They are the very first to read a new piece, to give notes and help me. I enjoy this process a lot. I invite them to the house every week to read them the pages I have just finished. We have a little cheese, cold cuts, peanuts, sandwiches, and wine. My wife Maria Eugenia ("Maru") always oversees this group. I trust her taste like no one else. She never bullshits me. She is harsh when need be and lets me know when things are heading in the right direction. I listen carefully to this group. I consider every note, even if I strongly disagree, because many times they're right. And they have no other agenda than to help me with their generosity and friendship. I think every writer must have a group like this and, more importantly, trust it.

Collaboration with my translator, Alan Page, is also very important in my writing process. Alan is a young poet who grew up between New York City and Mexico City. He is perfectly bilingual and has translated almost all of my work into English, including my novels and short stories. Because I'm not a native English-speaking writer, I need someone who will help me bring alive in English what I write. He has been the person who has made this possible. With him I have an intense dialogue trying to find the best way to make a sentence in English feel natural and organic. So Alan Page deserves a great deal of recognition in my work.

My team of agents and my lawyer are critical to my creative process as well. Keya Khayatian and Shana Eddy, my agents, and Linda Lichter, my lawyer, not only defend and support my work, they're among the first readers of everything I write. They helped me refine the screenplay, understand the kind of audience who is going to watch the film, and find the right people to produce and nurture it. All of these are creative matters, and I strongly consider the three of them part of my creative team.

Walter and Laurie gave the screenplay to several directors. Some of them I thought were completely wrong. Not because they were bad directors, but because they have a completely different aesthetic than mine and I was sure they wouldn't fully appreciate the project. In the end, I decided to propose myself as director. The first reaction of Walter and Laurie was "another writer wanting to turn director." I asked for a fair chance. I pitched the visualization, the casting, and the locations to them in order to be considered. I worked hard. Through the guidance of my old friend Alisa Tager, I began bringing them photos, maps, and ideas until I convinced them.

They quickly got a production company to support my first film as director: 2929 Productions. Shebnem Askin, Marc Butan, and the president of the company, Todd Wagner, decided to finance the film. And I will always thank them for doing so.

Next step: we needed an actress who could portray Sylvia and carry the film. We sent the screenplay to Charlize Theron. I've always considered her one of the greatest actresses of our time. Even though she is very young, she has already created such wonderful characters in her tremendous body of work. Her nominations and her Oscar are totally deserved. Fortunately for us, she said she wanted to meet me.

I was told I would only have one hour with her since she had a very tight schedule (she was doing dialog looping for *In The Valley of Elah*). We met at an Italian restaurant in Los Angeles. What was planned as one hour turned into almost five. Charlize is an intelligent, sensible woman, full of humor and occasional curses. I didn't let her go without getting her to commit to the film. She said "yes" with a big smile, and then she hugged me.

Charlize became the central part of the casting, the cornerstone that guided our casting choices. Every other character had to be selected around her. For example, Maria, her daughter, had to have some resemblance to her. And of course, young Mariana and Gina, her mother, needed to look a little bit like her.

Walter and Laurie brought Debbie Zane, the brilliant casting director, onto the project. Slowly we began to choose the right actors. The first day she sent me a tape from the first casting session with the actors she considered the three best girls for the character of Mariana and the three best guys for the character of Santiago. Without any doubt, even though it was the first day of casting, I chose Jennifer Lawrence and J. D. Pardo. I knew, deep in my heart, that these two kids were the right ones.

I have learned that casting should be based on three factors. The first one is talent, of course. The second is what the persona of the actor gives to the character—physical characteristics, ways of walking, ways of looking, background, etc. And third, and for me the most important, is taste. The way an actor chooses an emotion expresses his taste. I don't like actors that reinforce their acting by making faces or artificially raising their voices. I hate clichéd expressions. I like how good actors manage the physical distance with other actors, how they grab an object, when they decide to turn to look at the other actors. All of this cannot be registered intellectually, but more from the gut. Always an instinct. Too much rationalization, I think, spoils a casting selection. So I was sure that Jennifer and J. D. were absolutely the right choices.

Kim Basinger was suggested by Charlize. And right now I cannot see anyone else playing Gina. Kim played the part with such fragility and such strength at the same time. My friend Adrian Zurita, associate producer of the film and part of the group that helps me with my screenplays, was shocked when he saw Kim coming onto the set. "That is Gina" he exclaimed, "and I am already feeling sadness for the character." Introspective, silent, and elegantly discreet in person, Kim was able to open her emotions for the character in a way I would never have suspected. She elevated what was on the page.

The good thing about directing a film you have written is that you have had it in your head for years. I knew the kind of actors I needed and, also, the kind of locations. Since the four elements were fundamental to the story, the selection of the shooting locations and the visuals were extremely important.

I never do any research. I am not very good at it and I think that sometimes it takes away from the spontaneity of the writing. So I write about places that I have never been to before and have no idea how they really look, but I am certain in my imagination that they do exist. I began looking for the locations with a very clear image of what I had in mind. I had never been to New Mexico or Oregon before, but I was sure that in New Mexico I was going to be able to find an isolated desert plain and that in Oregon there would be a restaurant beside the cliffs.

I began traveling in New Mexico. First I was taken all around Albuquerque by the locations scouts. It was convenient for everyone: restaurants, equipment, hotels, crew, catering, all in one city. I refused. I thought the landscape was wrong. After traveling for miles and miles, I found Las Cruces, in the southern part of the state. It was perfect. It had the mood I needed, the landscape, the feeling of dust, and the contradiction between the Mexican and the American culture.

The same process took place in Oregon. The easy thing to do

would have been to shoot all of Sylvia's story in Portland, where there was a crew, film equipment, etc. Again, I refused. I thought the story really needed the sea, the cliffs, and the restaurant. We ended up shooting a great part of it in the remote Depoe Bay, almost three hours from Portland.

All of these choices meant less shooting days. Ray Angelic, one of the executive producers, asked me if it was worth sacrificing almost eight shooting days in order to have these locations. I was absolutely sure it was. And I hope after watching the film that the viewers agree.

Sacrificing these shooting days meant I had to severely cut the screenplay. Through the very painful process of taking out scenes, I tried to pare the story to the bare bones. Even intending for the audience to fill in information gaps, at one point I thought cutting these scenes would take it to an extreme. But there was no other way to do it if we wanted to make our shooting schedule.

Even after I cut nearly 20 percent of the screenplay, Phil Hardage, my good friend and the best first assistant director I had ever met, scheduled the film for fifty-five shooting days. But Ray Angelic had some bad news: we had only budgeted for forty days. It looked like an impossible task. This was a film that was intended to be shot in completely different locations, and that had a gigantic explosion, a plane accident, a twelve-year difference between stories, period costumes and sets, etc.

I sat down with Phil and with the brilliant director of photography Robert Elswit. They told me that it would be extremely difficult to make it, but that it was possible. So we decided to go for it. And I must say that without them and all the other filmmakers, without their experience, generosity and help, we would never have made it.

Another thing I learned in filmmaking is that the more you prep the film, the better. All the preparatory questions must be asked before you arrive on the set. But in my case another problem arose: my work permit. Since I am Mexican and didn't have a work permit for the United States, the producers decided not to begin preproduction until after my permit was issued. And because of Charlize's and Kim's schedule, we absolutely needed to start shooting the first week in November. I couldn't begin prepping properly until three weeks before shooting. Suddenly everything was compressed into just twenty days: costumes, construction, rehearsals, shooting lists, storyboards. I had to deal with the worst-case scenario for a first-time director: most of the questions had to be solved on set in the midst of shooting.

I can say that despite the time constraints, I am very pleased with the overall results. We did have a major difficulty with one scene in the film that was originally written differently from how it ended up being shot. This was the scene where John follows and confronts Sylvia and the Young Man. In the original version, Sylvia and the Young Man leave on a motorcycle and John chases them in his truck until they have a very dumb accident. However, this would have been very dangerous to shoot. On the Oregon coast, the wind can attain great force and the rain never, but never, stops in winter. So we cancelled that scene and we came up with an alternative, still utilizing the usual wind and rain. But, and this is a big "but," that day it didn't rain and there was a splendid sun. The weather in Oregon just wasn't cooperating, so we ended up improvising. To me, the scene seems a bit strained and even weird, but hopefully it works. Thankfully I have Craig Wood editing this film. His passion, his taste, and his knowledge were fundamental in telling this story.

There were some basic decisions I made from the very beginning. First all, I asked everyone to refer to *The Burning Plain* as "our film." Not my film, but ours. Second, I vowed never to use video monitors, but to direct sitting beside the camera, trying to establish the closest possible relationship with the actors. Third, I was willing to accept that at times I didn't know. This became a great tool, "I don't know." And the great thing about directing, as opposed to writing, is that you can always turn to someone and ask for help.

I most say that I was extremely lucky. I was surrounded by the best team possible. Not a crew, but a group of filmmakers in every area, behind and in front of camera. I never met a group of artists so committed to a film. They fought hard for our film.

I enjoyed directing like few things in my life. It is like being on a gigantic playground with great friends to play with. In my case, the best friends possible. It was a tough shoot, yes, but it was never overwhelming or stressful.

I am personally very happy with the film. Until now it has caused almost schizophrenic reviews from the critics. Either it is a great film or simply a very bad one. I like the fact that people react to it, and even though the negative critique hurts a lot, I love these strong reactions. It means that our film works: it causes controversy; it provokes feelings and raises emotions. This means that it is a living thing. And there is nothing better for a film than to have a life of its own.

—July 2009

The Burning Plain

Written By

Guillermo Arriaga

White October 8, 2007
Blue Revisions October 16, 2007
Pink Revisions October 22, 2007
Yellow Revisions October 30, 2007
Green Revisions November 15, 2007

Translation By
Alan Page

THE BURNING PLAIN (November 1, 2007)

Guillermo Arriaga

1   EXT. NEW MEXICO DESERT -- DAY   1

Five o'clock in the afternoon in the boundless desert. In
the middle of a lonely plain, a trailer home is burning.

The blaze crackles in the distance. The house is being rapidly
consumed. Flames lick out of the windows.

There is nothing, no one to be seen. The house is on fire.

2   INT. ROOM, SYLVIA'S APARTMENT -- MORNING   2

Dawn. A studio apartment, with everything crammed into one
place: the bed, the living room, the dining room, the
kitchenette. The room has been painted an ocean blue. The
furniture is elegant: a leather couch, a rocking chair, a
small wooden table, and four wooden chairs.

At one end of the room is a bed. A naked man: John (39),
sleeps deeply. Beside him, Sylvia (30), also naked, stares
at him silently. She is blonde, thin; her elegant beauty
starkly contrasts with John. She shakes him.

                    SYLVIA
          Get up.

The man slightly wakes up.

                    JOHN
          What?

                    SYLVIA
          We fall sleep again.

The man opens his eyes and looks up at her.

                    JOHN
          Just give me five more minutes please.

                    SYLVIA
          No, get out.

She looks at him for a moment, gets up and walks out naked
to the balcony. He sits up, picks his pants up off the floor
and sits on a chair to put them on. He is a big man, a little
heavy, with deep bags under his blue eyes.

3   EXT. BALCONY, SYLVIA'S HOUSE -- DAY   3

The balcony opens onto a suburb of a city at the edge of a
river in Oregon. The buildings are illuminated by the sun
rising out of the east.

The sky is a leaden blue and some clouds float over the
horizon. We hear the sounds of voices and traffic in the
distance.

Sylvia leans on the rail to watch the river.

4   EXT. STREET, CITY -- DAY   4

Two local women (35) are walking their sons (10&8) to school.
One of the kids turns to look up at the balcony and stares
at the beautiful, naked woman.

The women look up and see her. They yank the boys and turn
their heads away. The women hurry their kids along.

5   EXT. BALCONY, SYLVIA'S HOUSE -- DAY   5

Sylvia seems oblivious to the scene she caused. She grabs a
pack of cigarettes from the table and lights one.

Through the curtains, she watches the man leave, slamming
the door.

Calmly, Sylvia gives the cigarette a long drag and stares
into the distance.

6   EXT. STREETS, CITY -- DAY   6

Sylvia walks out into the street. The buildings downtown can
be seen in the distance. It's a quiet area, a middle-class
neighborhood that's starting to get hip. Boutiques,
restaurants and bars have begun to populate the blocks.

Sylvia is wearing a simple blue cotton dress with her hair
let down. Her figure shows through the fabric. She walks
down the street.

Carlos (35), a wiry Mexican, watches her from the moment she
steps out of the house. He has a coffee in one hand and a
doughnut in the other.

Sylvia walks toward the corner. Carlos follows her with his
eyes, from a distance. Sylvia feels his presence and turns
toward him. They exchange glances for a few moments. Carlos
stares at her until she sees a Honda Civic pulling up beside
her. She gets in.

7   INT. LAURA'S CAR -- DAY   7

Laura (33) drives. She has a pleasant face and a body
intensely curvaceous.

               LAURA
    Hi.

               SYLVIA
    Hey.

8   EXT. STREET, SYLVIA'S APARTMENT -- DAY   8

From the corner Carlos observes the car driving down the
street. He walks to an Ikon parked in the parking lot behind
him, gets in and follows them.

9   INT. LAURA'S CAR -- DAY   9

Laura drives and turns to look at Sylvia.

               LAURA
    Late night?

               SYLVIA
    Yeah, I guess.

               LAURA
    Again?

               SYLVIA
    Yeah, again.

               LAURA
    Same guy?

Sylvia shakes her head.

               SYLVIA
    No.

               LAURA
    Do I know him?

Sylvia shrugs her shoulders.

               SYLVIA
    Maybe.

               LAURA
    Do you know him?

(CONTINUED)

9   CONTINUED: 9

Both smile. Laura continues driving.

> LAURA (CONT'D)
> How do you do it? No matter how hard
> I try, they won't give me the time
> of day.

> SYLVIA
> This one's an old flame.

Laura smiles again.

9A   EXT. ROAD, OREGON'S COAST -- DAY   9A

The Civic drives on the road, close to the edge of the sea.

10   EXT. WILLY'S -- DAY   10

The Civic drives into a restaurant parking lot that stands
alone at the edge of a mountain covered in extremely tall
trees. The restaurant is overlooking a small bay just off
Pacific Highway 1 at the foot of an enormous cliff.

The restaurant has been built out of wood, with large windows
looking out at the dark sea. Laura and Sylvia get out of the
car and enter.

Carlos's Ikon passes by them in the road.

11   INT. WILLY'S KITCHEN -- DAY   11

Sylvia goes into the kitchen. Several cooks are hard at work.
One of them greets her respectfully.

> COOK
> Good morning.

> SYLVIA
> Hey...good morning.

12   INT. KITCHEN, RESTAURANT -- MORNING   12

Sylvia goes into the chef working station and walks up to
Lawrence, the head chef.

> SYLVIA
> What are the specials today?

The chef gestures toward various pots.

(CONTINUED)

12   CONTINUED: 12

                          LAWRENCE
                Lobster in a white wine sauce, haddock
                with spinach and almonds, seafood
                linguini in a tomato sauce.

Sylvia smiles wryly.

                          SYLVIA
                Twenty five no shows from last night's
                wedding?

They both smile. She looks at the dishes and turns to leave.
On her way out she runs into John - one of the chefs. They
exchange a glance and Sylvia keeps walking into the
restaurant.

12A   INT. WILLY'S -- DAY   12A

The place is still empty. It is an elegant restaurant. The
tables have linen tablecloths, silver cutlery, designer
dishes. The waiters, impeccably dressed, arrange the tables.

Sylvia stands at the door, supervising the action.

13   INT. WILLY'S -- DAY   13

It's noon. The restaurant is full. Sylvia is the maitre d'
and runs the place efficiently. She welcomes a couple of
customers in their sixties at the door who are guided by
Sophie (24), the hostess, a beautiful girl.

                          SYLVIA
                Welcome back Mr. and Mrs. Evans,
                it's so nice to see you again. Do
                you remember Sophie? She will take
                you to your usual table. I hope you
                enjoy your meal.

She turns to Sophie.

                          SOPHIE
                Follow me.

Sophie guides the couple to their table. Another waitress,
Vivi (26), approaches Sylvia.

                          VIVI
                Sylvia, table six needs some help
                with wine.

She points at a table where four young men are eating lunch.
Sylvia walks toward them.

                                              (CONTINUED)

13   CONTINUED: 13

They're dressed in expensive suits, Rolex watches, hand made
Italian shoes: showy stockbrokers.

                    SYLVIA
          Good afternoon, Vivi told me you
          need a wine recommendation.

One of them, handsome and confident, smiles at her. He is
reading the wine list.

                    YOUNG MAN
          We're having the Petit Filet.

                    SYLVIA
          I suggest '87 Chateau Castés Bordeaux.

                    YOUNG MAN
          I haven't heard of it.

The young man checks the list.

                    SYLVIA
          It is not in our list. We have it
          downstairs in our reserve.

                    YOUNG MAN
          Oh thank you. That will be fantastic.

                    SYLVIA
          I will be right back.

She turns and walks to the kitchen. The young man smiles to
his friends.

14   INT. FRONT DESK, WILLY'S -- DAY   14

The restaurant is almost empty. Only the young stockbrokers
and a couple remain in the place.

Sylvia walks over to Laura at the front desk.

                    SYLVIA
          I'm going out for a quick cigarette
          ok?

15   EXT. CLIFF -- DAY   15

Sylvia sits alone on the rocks, watching the waves crash
beside her. She is lost in thought.

She grabs a rock and lifts up her skirt. Her knee shows
several scars.

                                              (CONTINUED)

15   CONTINUED: 15

She starts rubbing the rock against her knee until it bleeds.

She digs into the wound to make it bleed a little more.
Then she walks up to the water's edge, scoops up some water
and cleans off the blood.

She takes her things and gets up to leave.

16   EXT. PATH, CLIFF -- DAY   16

She starts down the narrow path that winds up the cliff. It
is a dangerous route. Suddenly Sylvia stops, walks toward a
large, jutting rock and stands on the very edge with the sea
just beyond, crashing furiously below.

Sylvia looks as if she is about to jump. She opens her arms
and leans slightly forward. She remains like this for a
moment. The wind shakes her hair, and she sways.

Sylvia looks at the raging ocean and walks away.

17   EXT. WILLY'S -- DAY   17

Sylvia returns to the restaurant. The four young men to whom
she recommended the wine are leaving. One of them walks up
to Sylvia.

                    YOUNG MAN
          Great suggestion, that Chateau Castés.

                    SYLVIA
          It's one of my favorites.

                    YOUNG MAN
          And which red would you recommend?

                    SYLVIA
          It depends on the meal.

The young man smiles at her answer.

                    YOUNG MAN
          Well, you can figure that out when I
          buy you dinner.

                    SYLVIA
          I don't date customers.

                    YOUNG MAN
          I'm done with lunch, I'm not your
          customer anymore.

                                        (CONTINUED)

17   CONTINUED: 17

Sylvia looks at him: he's handsome and confident.

                         SYLVIA
            Come pick me up in one hour.

18   INT. KITCHEN, RESTAURANT -- CONTINUOUS   18

From a window, John watches Sylvia flirt with the young man.
He stares at her furiously.

19   EXT. STREETS, CITY -- EVENING   19

Carlos watches, leaning against a car parked on the sidewalk
opposite Sylvia's apartment. He smokes, vigilant.

A Ducati motorcycle pulls up before Sylvia's apartment
building. Sylvia and the young man dismount. Both take off
their helmets. Carlos watches. Sylvia spots him and they
exchange a glance.

The young man and Sylvia enter the small building.

20   INT. ROOM, SYLVIA'S HOUSE -- NIGHT   20

Sylvia is fucking the young man. He is on top, concentrating.
She lies under him, staring elsewhere, completely abstracted.
It seems as if she is there just to be there.

The sex act continues, and the longer it goes on, the further
away Sylvia seems to be.

21   EXT. NEW MEXICO DESERT 1993 -- DAY   21

A run-down 1982 Chevrolet pickup drives down a path kicking
up a dustcloud. Some jackrabbits jump out of its way.

22   INT. PICKUP TRUCK -- DAY   22

Behind the wheel is Cristobal (18), a blond chicano dressed
in a cowboy hat and white shirt. In the middle is Xavier
(18), and on the other side is Cristobal's brother Santiago
(17), dark-skinned, clear-eyed, taciturn and quiet. The three
travel in silence, listening to some Tex Mex music.

Cristobal drives aggressively, barely dodging potholes and
shrubs. In the distance we can see the ruins of the burning
trailer home.

                         CRISTOBAL
            It's over there.

Santiago raises his head and looks at it for a long time.

23   EXT. NEW MEXICO DESERT -- DAY   23

Cristobal parks the truck and the three get out. They walk
toward the house which is surrounded by yellow police tape.
It has been completely destroyed by the fire. The walls
stand charred and roofless, the tires burst, soot and ashes
everywhere.

Santiago seems most affected by the scene. He circles around
without taking his eyes off it.

Cristobal crosses the yellow tape and examines the place
leisurely.

                    CRISTOBAL
          Holy shit!

He picks up a rod warped by the heat and shows it to Xavier.

                    CRISTOBAL (CONT'D)
          The heat twisted up the metal. Look.

Santiago looks at him askance, taken aback by the comment.
He crosses the yellow tape and keeps looking through the
remains.

Cristobal hops through a heap of scattered blackened metal
and walks up to the house. He looks closely and sees a room
with a scorched bed.

Santiago and Xavier approach. Cristobal points.

                    CRISTOBAL (CONT'D)
          That's where my dad and that fuckin'
          slut burned.

Xavier looks into the room.

                    XAVIER
          How'd the fire start?

Cristobal shrugs.

                    CRISTOBAL
          The cops think they left the gas on
          and it exploded.

                    XAVIER
          So, it was an accident?

                    CRISTOBAL
          Yep, that's what the sheriff says.

                                        (CONTINUED)

23   CONTINUED: 23

Santiago, bewildered, silently examines the room.

> CRISTOBAL (CONT'D)
> They were fucking when they died.
> Their bodies got stuck together with
> the fire. They had to cut them apart
> with a knife.

Santiago looks at his brother suspiciously. Everything
Cristobal says seems to hurt him badly.

> XAVIER
> Who was the bitch?

> CRISTOBAL
> Some married woman from Maroma. This
> is where the motherfuckers met,
> halfway between both towns.

Santiago grabs onto the windowsill and jumps inside.

24   INT. BURNT TRAILER HOME -- CONTINUOUS   24

He stands before the black mattress as if trying to understand
what happened. Cristobal looks in.

> CRISTOBAL
> What the fuck are you doing?

Santiago stands pensively and then turns to Cristobal.

> SANTIAGO
> What do you think was going through
> dad's head while he was burning?

Cristobal twists his face into something like a smirk.

> CRISTOBAL
> Getting the fuck out.

Santiago, without taking his eyes from the charred bed,
answers his own question.

> SANTIAGO
> Maybe that he never went back to
> Mexico.

25   EXT. NEW MEXICO TOWN -- DAY   25

The truck parks in front of a humble wooden house on a dusty
street in a small town in New Mexico. Santiago gets out to
let Xavier out, who waves goodbye.

(CONTINUED)

25   CONTINUED: 25

                            XAVIER
                   Later.

26   INT. PICKUP TRUCK -- DAY   26

      The truck pulls away leaving Xavier behind. Santiago is
      visibly upset.

                            SANTIAGO
                   Why the fuck did you bring Xavier?

                            CRISTOBAL
                   'Cause he's my friend.

                            SANTIAGO
                   We bury dad tomorrow and you're
                   running a fucking circus.

      Cristobal stops the truck and turns to look at him.

                            CRISTOBAL
                   I ain't runnin' no circus, bitch. I
                   was just telling him what happened.

                            SANTIAGO
                   What the fuck for?

                            CRISTOBAL
                        (challenging)
                   'Cause I wanted to. You got a problem
                   with that?

                            SANTIAGO
                   Fuck you.

      He gets out and slams the door. Cristobal takes off.

27   EXT. STREET, TOWN -- DAY   27

      Santiago is left standing in the middle of the street.

28   EXT. SANTIAGO'S HOUSE -- DAY   28

      Santiago walks up to his house - a small town construction
      surrounded by a large plot of land fenced off with barbed
      wire. A mesquite grows in the middle of the plot. Several
      rusted farming tools lie strewn about the place. Toward the
      back, in the garage, is the truck. Santiago opens a metal
      door and walks onto the property.

      A white-winged dove sings on one of the mesquite's branches.
      Santiago sees it, pulls a slingshot from his pants, picks up

                                                        (CONTINUED)

28   CONTINUED: 28

a stone and aims. He lets it fly and hits the dove in the
chest. It flaps as it drops.

Santiago picks it up off the ground and twists its head off.
Blood shoots up in small squirts. He starts to pluck its
feathers off as he heads home.

29   INT. KITCHEN, SANTIAGO'S HOUSE -- DAY   29

He opens a screen door and steps into the kitchen. He finds
Ana (40), his mother, sitting at the kitchen table dressed
in blue jeans and a black t-shirt. Ana was once beautiful,
but her beauty has eroded under years of dust.

Next to Ana are her sisters, Paula (38) and Rebecca (37),
both also worn-down beauties. Before them is a bottle of
expensive whiskey, half-empty glasses and ashtrays
overflowing.

The three grow quiet when they notice Santiago.

                    SANTIAGO
          Hey Mom. Hey aunt Paula, Rebecca.

Her mother stares at him.

                    ANA
          Did you fight with Cristobal?

                    SANTIAGO
          No.

                    ANA
          I don't want any fighting. Now more
          than ever. Do you hear me?

Santiago nods and looks his mother in the eye for a moment.
He guts the bird, pulls out the last clumps of feathers and
washes it in the sink.

                    ANA (CONT'D)
          And stop killing doves 'cause they're
          nesting.

                    SANTIAGO
          'Kay.

He sets the dove on a plate and puts it into the fridge. He
turns around and points at the bottle of whiskey on the table.

                    SANTIAGO (CONT'D)
          That's my dad's whiskey.

                                                    (CONTINUED)

29 CONTINUED: 29

Ana looks at him angrily.

                         ANA
             Is it? And when the hell is he gonna
             drink it?

Santiago says nothing else and walks out of the kitchen.

30   INT. SANTIAGO AND CRISTOBAL'S ROOM -- NIGHT   30

Cristobal is playing video games on a computer. Santiago
lies on his bed reading some magazines. Through the window
we can see the desert lit by the moon.

We hear shouts and laughter from the three women. Cristobal
lifts up his head, pricking up his ear.

                         CRISTOBAL
             Mom's drunk again.

Santiago reads on for a bit and, without looking, answers.

                         SANTIAGO
             What'd you expect?

The brothers remain silent and Santiago keeps reading.

31   EXT. SANTIAGO'S HOUSE -- DAY   31

Several cars are parked outside the house. Some mourners
mill about. Santiago and Cristobal, each dressed in a black
suit, walk amidst the people.

Paula emerges dressed in black and walks toward the brothers.

                         PAULA
             Santiago and Cristobal, c'mere...

She takes them to a corner of the property. The rest of the
mourners begin to walk towards their cars.

32   EXT. SANTIAGO'S HOUSE -- DAY   32

They arrive at a spot by the garage. Paula looks hung over.
You cannot see the look in her eyes through her sunglasses.

                         PAULA
             Your mom ain't going to the funeral.

Santiago and Cristobal seem like they expected this.

                                              (CONTINUED)

32 CONTINUED: 32

> PAULA (CONT'D)
> Me and Rebecca ain't goin' either.
> The son of a bitch doesn't deserve
> it.

Santiago turns to look at her angrily.

> SANTIAGO
> He never did anything to you.

Paula smiles sardonically.

> PAULA
> Don't you get it? You're the one he
> really fucked up.
>   (a beat)
> Take care of everything, the both of
> you.

33 EXT. TOWN CEMETERY -- DAY   33

The cemetery is very small, at the edge of the town. It's
hard to say where the cemetery ends and the desert begins.
Herbs and cacti grow among the graves, some of them so damaged
that the earth sinks into them. Bones, dust and rocks are
all one.

All the mourners stand around the open grave. There are no
more than fifteen and a town priest. No pomp. Just some dirt
shoveled and a silent goodbye.

Further off, at the edge of the cemetery, Robert, a blond
man, six foot five and solid, is surrounded by four equally
blond teenagers: two girls and two boys who watch the funeral.

Cristobal notices the family and points it out to Xavier.

> CRISTOBAL
> Who are they?

> XAVIER
> Don't know.

34 EXT. TOWN CEMETERY -- LATER   34

The burial is over and the mourners make their way out. As
Santiago and Cristobal walk past the family, the blond man
confronts them and glares with his reddened blue eyes.

> ROBERT
> I hope your father is rotting in
> hell.

34 CONTINUED: 34

Cristobal and Santiago are taken aback. They are speechless.

                    ROBERT (CONT'D)
          That wetback piece of shit took away
          the best thing I ever had.

The priest overhears this and tries to calm him down.

                    PRIEST
          Hey! Leave the boys alone.

Robert, blind with rage, faces him.

                    ROBERT
          Alone?
               (He points at his
                children.)
          It's their father's fault that my
          kids lost their mother.

He turns to Santiago and Cristobal.

                    ROBERT (CONT'D)
          I hope you rot too.

He turns to leave. His children stand dumbstruck for a moment
and then follow their father. All except Mariana (16) - slim,
with an ageless face and green eyes - whose gaze meets with
Santiago's just as she leaves.

35 INT. HANGAR, LANDING STRIP, TAMAULIPAS -- DAY   35

In one of the sides of the hangar there's a wall decorated
with a large map of Mexico, and furnished with a table and
four chairs, Santiago (30), dressed in jeans and a khaki
shirt, plays dominoes with Carlos and other pilots.

An operator (30), a woman with green eyes and a pilot's
jacket, is sitting in a desk attending to a short wave radio
with headphones on.

Carlos puts a domino in the table.

                    CARLOS
          Te vas compadre. [You can win with
          this one, compadre.]

The other pilot knocks his domino in the table.

                    PILOT 1
          Paso. [I pass.]

                                                    (CONTINUED)

Santiago puts his last domino.

>   CARLOS
>   Me voy, ganamos. [I'm done, we won.]

The operator talks to someone in the radio. She turns to
the pilots playing.

>   OPERATOR
>   Hay un trabajo en Los Aztecas ¿quién
>   lo toma? [There's a job in Los
>   Aztecas? Who takes it?]

Carlos leaves the table and goes to make himself a cup of
coffee while he speaks to the operator holding the microphone
of the short wave radio.

>   SANTIAGO
>   ¿Cuánto pagan? [How much do they
>   pay?]

The operator holds down the button to speak over the radio.

>   OPERATOR
>   ¿A cuánto la hectárea? [How much per
>   hectare?]

The operator hears the answer and turns to Santiago.

>   OPERATOR (CONT'D)
>   500 pesos. Son ochocientas hectáreas.
>   [500 pesos. It's eight hundred
>   hectares.]

Santiago turns toward Carlos (35) - also dressed in a khaki
shirt - who nods. Santiago turns to the operator.

>   SANTIAGO
>   Ok. Nosotros lo tomamos. [Ok, we'll
>   take it.]

The operator grabs the mic.

>   OPERATOR
>   El piloto va para allá. [The pilot's
>   on his way.]

Carlos takes the cup of coffee that Santiago so painstakingly
prepared, and takes it with him, leaving Santiago coffeeless.

36   EXT. RUSTIC HANGARS, TAMAULIPAS -- DAY   36

From behind a hangar, Maria (12) - tall, light brown-skinned
with green eyes - jumps rope with some girls her age. A woman
is sitting on a chair, knitting, watching on them.

Santiago, walking toward the land strip, shouts at María.

                    SANTIAGO
          Maria ven. [Maria, come here.]

Maria doesn't pay attention and keeps on playing.

                    MARIA
          Voy. [Going.]

                    SANTIAGO
          María, vamonos. [Maria, let`s go.]

The woman turns to María.

                    WOMAN
          Ándale Maria que te busca tu papá.
          [Come on Maria, your dad's looking
          for you.]

María drops the rope and turns to her friends.

                    MARIA
          Nos vemos al rato. [See ya.]

She runs toward her father who is already close to his crop
duster plane in the landing strip.

37   EXT. LANDING STRIP -- DAY   37

Four crop dusters are parked on the strip. The sun throbs on
the asphalt. Santiago and Carlos are checking the airplane's
wings and flaps. Maria arrives running.

                    MARIA
          Hi daddy, what's up?

                    SANTIAGO
          Hey honey, we got a job.

                    MARIA
          Can I stay with my friends?

                    SANTIAGO
          Sorry sweetie, we gotta go.

                                        (CONTINUED)

37   CONTINUED: 37

                         MARIA
                  Please.

                         SANTIAGO
                  No hija. [No sweetheart.]

                         MARIA
                  Ándale por favor. [Come on, please.]

Carlos sneaks up behind her and pokes her ribs.

                         CARLOS
                      (Mocking her)
                  Ándale por favor. [Come on, please.]

                         MARIA
                  !Ya! [Stop it!]

                         CARLOS
                  ¿Cómo que ya chamaca? Deje de estar
                  de rezongona. Ándele a trabajar.
                  [Stop it? You stop nagging and now
                  let`s got to work.]

Carlos opens the copilot's door and gestures for Maria to
get in.

38   INT. CROP DUSTER -- DAY   38

The crop duster moves down the runway. Santiago sits in the
pilot seat. Beside him, Carlos checks the instruments.
They are forced to shout over the noise of the propeller.

                         SANTIAGO
                  Do you have the coordinates?

                         MARIA
                  Yeah, I just put them into the GPS.

Santiago gives her a thumbs up. They gather speed and take
off. As they rise, Maria stares at the long fields of sorghum
stretching below her.

39   EXT. SKY -- DAY   39

The plane plows through the bright, hot sky. Below them
stretch out the immense, beautiful parcels sown with mature
sorghum; its stalks cover the horizon in an intense orange.

40   INT. CROP DUSTER -- DAY   40

Maria examines the coordinates on the GPS and after a while points below her.

> MARIA
> Este es el rancho. [That's the ranch.]

Santiago turns and locates the rustic landing strip made of packed dirt from among the orange-green rows of sorghum. Santiago tilts and descends.

41   EXT. RUSTIC LANDING STRIP -- DAY   41

A Ford 2005 pickup truck sits parked beside the runway. Two fat and sweaty ranchers in their forties await the arrival of the crop duster as it approaches to land.

The plane lands softly and stops a few yards away from the truck. Santiago turns it around to face the ranchers, who walk over as soon as the propeller settles.

Santiago, Carlos and Maria get out. One of the ranchers goes to shake Santiago and Carlos's hand.

> RANCHER
> Buenas tardes. [Good afternoon.]

> SANTIAGO
> (In a slight accent)
> Buenas. ['Afternoon.]

> RANCHER
> Necesitamos que fumigue ese lado del
> rancho. Ya sacamos a los trabajadores
> y no queda nadie en las tierras. [We
> need you to dust this side of the
> ranch. We pulled all the workers
> out, so the lands are all clear.]

Rancher 2 points toward a truck with chemicals parked in the other side of the road.

> RANCHER 2
> Ahí están los químicos. [There are
> the chemicals.]

Carlos turns to Santiago.

> CARLOS
> Voy a checarlos. [I'm going to check
> them.]

(CONTINUED)

41   CONTINUED: 41

He walks to the chemicals' truck. Rancher 1 points out a
little shack in the distance.

                    RANCHER
          Ahí hay estufa y pueden encontrar
          Maseca para tortillas. ¿Necesitan
          algo más? [There's a stove in there,
          with corn flour to make tortillas.
          D'you need anything else?]

                    SANTIAGO
          No gracias, nosotros nos arreglamos.
          [No thanks, we'll manage.]

                    RANCHER
          Nos vemos pues. [See you later then.]

They say goodbye and the fat ranchers hop in the pickup truck.

42   EXT. RUSTIC LANDING STRIP -- DAY   42

Santiago checks the plane to make sure everything is in order,
while Carlos pours the chemicals into the dusting tank.

                    CARLOS
          ¿Quién fumiga primero? [Who goes
          first?]

                    SANTIAGO
          Va un volado. [We'll flip for it.]

Santiago takes out a coin.

                    CARLOS
          ¿Águila o Sol? [Heads or tails?]

                    SANTIAGO
          Aguila. [Tails.]

Santiago flips it up in the air. The coin drops: tails. Carlos
looks disgusted.

                    CARLOS
          Mejor empieza tú. [Better you go
          first.]

Santiago smiles at him.

43   EXT. RUSTIC LANDING STRIP -- DAY   43

The plane's engines are running. Santiago is in the pilot's
seat. At the edge of the runway, Maria shouts at him.

                                              (CONTINUED)

43   CONTINUED: 43

                              MARIA
                    I'll wait for you over there.

She points at the shack in the distance. Santiago gives her
a thumbs up, drives the plane down to one end of the runway.

44   EXT. SORGHUM FIELDS, TAMAULIPAS -- DAY   44

The crop duster sprays the fields. Its wheels knock against
the tallest stalks of sorghum.

The vast orange expanse is crossed again and again by white-
winged doves that scatter as the crop duster sprays close to
the ground.

45   EXT. SHACK -- DAY   45

Carlos and Maria, carrying a shopping bag, walk away from
the landing strip and arrive at the shack. There is a rusted
bicycle leaning against the wall. Carlos points at it.

                          CARLOS
                    Voy al pueblo a comprar algo de comer
                    en esa bicicleta. [I'm going out to
                    town on that bike to get us something
                    to eat.]

                          MARIA
                    Yo mientras voy haciendo unas
                    tortillas. [I'll make some tortillas
                    in the meantime.]

Carlos pedals away as Maria heads toward the shack.

46   EXT. SORGHUM FIELDS, TAMAULIPAS -- DAY   46

The plane flies low overhead. Santiago is an expert and does
his work impeccably.

47   INT. SHACK -- DAY   47

Maria dexterously kneads the corn flour and makes some
tortillas. Through the window we can see the crop duster
spraying in the distance.

48   EXT. PATH -- DAY   48

An '82 Chevrolet pickup truck is parked on a lonely path in
the New Mexico desert, surrounded by giant saguaros, chollas,
sotol plants, mesquite trees and yuccas. The heat and dust
seem to devour everything.

49   INT. TRUCK -- CONTINUOUS   49

Nick Martínez (42), tall, with thin features, light skin,
longish hair and glasses, waits while listening to music.
He sweats and, every now and again, has a swig of Coors.
Below, at the feet of the passenger seat, he has a full
cooler.

It's clear he's been waiting for a long time. He looks both
ways: there is nothing, nobody, just the vast, boiling plain.

Suddenly, we see a '80 Ford Pinto barrel down a dirt path.

50   EXT. PATH -- DAY   50

The Ford Pinto parks next to the truck. The driver is Gina
(39) - a blond with remote nordic genes: light hair, blue
eyes, freckles and a worn-down, though still seductive body.

Nick walks toward her. She has the window rolled down.

                    GINA
          Sorry I'm late, but Robert just
          wouldn't leave for work.

                    NICK
          Don't worry about it.

Nick's accent still has a hint of Mexican.

                    NICK (CONT'D)
          Can I get you a beer?

She nods. Nick goes to his truck, opens the passenger door
and pulls out the cooler. He takes a beer and brings it to
her. She opens it without getting out of the car, puts the
bottle cap in her shirt pocket and looks around.

                    GINA
          Did you make sure nobody's around?

Nick nods. Gina sighs.

                    GINA (CONT'D)
          I feel real strange doing this.

                    NICK
          Me too.

A silence.

                                              (CONTINUED)

50   CONTINUED: 50

                              NICK (CONT'D)
                    'Bout what time d'you have to get
                    back?

                              GINA
                    I've got to be in Maroma at six.

Again, silence. A coyote appears a few yards away and stares
at them. The coyote trots off and Nick leans on Gina's car.

                              NICK
                    D'you want me to get in?

She nods. She unlocks the passenger door.

51   INT. GINA'S CAR -- DAY   51

Nick gets in. They are silent again. He reaches out and
brushes against her leg. She lightly strokes his finger.

                              GINA
                    I'm scared to death.

She squeezes Nick's hand. She looks very nervous.

                              NICK
                    D'you want us to leave it for some
                    other day?

She shakes her head.

                              GINA
                    No, that's ok...
                         (A beat)
                    D'you love me?

                              NICK
                    I've loved you for months.

He strokes her face. She catches his hand between her neck
and shoulder. She stares through the windshield when suddenly
she grabs him by the neck and kisses him slowly. They start
to make out.

He puts his hand on her breast and she pulls it away. He
tries again, and she does the same.

                              GINA
                    Not there...please...

She grabs Nick's hand and moves it down to her inner thigh.
Nick rubs her. They start to get turned on.

                                        (CONTINUED)

51   CONTINUED: 51

She stops, nervous and glances every which way.

                    GINA (CONT'D)
          You're sure there's no one around?

Nick holds his breath: he is really hot.

                    NICK
          One of my cousins lent me this place.
          I haven't been there, but my cousin
          told me is far away from everything.
          You wanna go?

52   EXT. TRAILER HOME -- DAY   52

They drive up in Gina's Pinto and park before a trailer home
in the middle of the desert.

53   OMITTED   53

54   INT. TRAILER HOME -- DAY   54

They walk in. The place is a mess. Empty glasses, ashtrays
spilling over, dirty napkins, open bottles. A Remington
pump-action shotgun, all rusty, lies on one of the sofas.
Burnt-out 12 caliber shells lie strewn about: the place is a
disaster. Gina stands in the middle of the room, watching.
Nick hugs her from behind and kisses her neck.

                    NICK
          It ain't no Hilton.

He grabs her hand and leads her into the bedroom.

55   INT. BEDROOM, TRAILER HOME -- DAY   55

Another mess: the bed unmade, bottles of beer lying about
the carpet, the sheets in a bunch and the acrid stench of
old cigarette smoke.

Nick opens the blinds and windows. Gina sits on the bed.
Nick sits down beside her. They start to kiss. Hurriedly,
Nick gets naked. He starts to take off Gina's pants. She
allows this, but as soon as Nick tries to take off her blouse,
she stops him and shakes her head.

Nick looks at her, puzzled, but continues. She is left naked
from the waist down: her body bears the traces of four
pregnancies. Gina climbs on top of him and they start to
make love.

56   INT. KITCHEN, GINA'S HOUSE -- NIGHT   56

Mariana (16), is making her younger brothers some dinner.
The scene is all bickering and commotion. Bobby (10,) a rosy-
cheeked blond kid, demands his dinner.

                        BOBBY
            I want cereal, Mariana.

Mariana, who is frying some eggs for Monnie (8), turns around
to tend to him. The eggs begin to burn.

                        MONNIE
            I want my eggs over easy.

                        MARIANA
            Well, that's real sad luck for you,
            'cause you're gettin' them well done.

She drops them on the plate and Monnie pushes them away in
disgust. Pat (14), walks in with three friends and opens the
refrigerator.

                        PAT
            Mariana, what's for dinner?

                        MARIANA
            You can fix you and your friends
            some cereal.

Pat and his friends take out some milk and dishes. We hear
the noise of a car. Mariana looks out and sees Gina, her
mother, parking the Pinto. Monnie breaks her concentration.

                        MONNIE
            The eggs taste yucky.

Mariana sighs, annoyed. Gina walks into the house, hurried.
She leaves some supermarket bags on the floor.

                        GINA
                    (To Mariana)
            Everything ok sweetie?

Mariana nods uninterested. Gina starts making excuses.

                        GINA (CONT'D)
            The supermarket was packed. I mean,
            the lines went round the aisles.

                        MONNIE
            Mommy, Mariana made me a stinky egg.

                                            (CONTINUED)

56   CONTINUED: 56

                          GINA
                Then don't eat it honey, I'll make
                you another one. Did your daddy call?

                          MARIANA
                Yeah, he said he'd be home tomorrow.
                He's making a delivery in Abilene.

Gina turns to fry up some more eggs. Mariana grabs the box
of cereal and sits down to eat.

57   INT. LIVING ROOM, GINA'S HOUSE -- NIGHT   57

The house is quiet. We can only hear the sound of the
television that Mariana watches, alone.

Gina stands in the door.

                          GINA
                Mariana, it's bedtime hon.

Mariana indolently turns to look at her.

                          MARIANA
                As soon as my show is over.

                          GINA
                All right now, but no later than
                that. G'night.

Mariana waves goodbye and Gina walks off to her room.

58   INT. BEDROOM, GINA'S HOUSE -- NIGHT   58

Gina sits on a stool, looking at herself in a peeling mirror
as she takes off her makeup. Her face shows joy, confusion,
sadness.

When she starts to unbutton her blouse, she feels something
in her pocket: it's the beer bottle cap Nick gave her. She
looks at it for a moment, squeezes it in her hand, opens a
drawer an takes out a box. She hides the bottle cap inside
the box and puts the box back in its place.

59   EXT. WILLY'S -- DAY   59

It's early in the morning. The DUCATI Motorcycle pulls up
before the restaurant.

60   INT. KITCHEN, RESTAURANT -- DAY   60

John watches everything from the window. He loses his
composure as soon as he sees Sylvia kiss the driver goodbye.

61   INT. WILLY'S -- DAY   61

Sylvia enters the restaurant. She greets Laura at the cashier.

                    SYLVIA
          Hey.

                    LAURA
          Hi Sylvia.

                    SYLVIA
          Any news?

                    LAURA
          Senator Parkes's office called. He's
          coming with a party of ten for lunch.
          His secretary asked if we can serve
          them bouillabaisse, steamed
          langoustines, tuna sashimi and
          chocolate souffle.

                    SYLVIA
          Shit, would it kill them to give us
          a day head's up?

62   INT. KITCHEN, RESTAURANT -- DAY   62

Sylvia enters the kitchen and heads straight for Lawrence.

                    SYLVIA
          Lawrence, Senator Parkes is coming
          in two hours. He asked for the usual
          stuff.

                    LAWRENCE
          In two hours? Where does he expect
          me to get everything?

                    SYLVIA
          I will call Mr. Forster, from the
          Fish Market. He owes me a few favors.

She heads off, but John catches up with her in the hallway.

63   INT. HALLWAY, RESTAURANT -- DAY   63

                      JOHN
            Sylvia.

                      SYLVIA
            What's up?

                      JOHN
            Where were you last night?

                      SYLVIA
            Home.

                      JOHN
            With who?

                      SYLVIA
            You promised never to ask questions.

                      JOHN
            Who the fuck with?

                      SYLVIA
            We've got work to do, excuse me.

      She walks around him and returns to the restaurant.

64   INT. WILLY'S -- DAY   64

      The place is full again. Senator Parkes and his people are
      sitting at a table. Sylvia tends to them.

                      SYLVIA
            Sophie, the senator's wife has an
            empty glass. Offer her more wine.

      Sophie carries out Sylvia's request. Then she turns to Vivi.

                      SYLVIA (CONT'D)
            Vivi, go ask the kitchen how the
            chocolate soufflé is going.

65   EXT. WILLY'S -- DAY   65

      Hiding in the trees outside, Carlos discreetly watches the
      restaurant through its large windows.

66   INT. WILLY'S -- AFTERNOON   66

      The restaurant is empty. Sophie, Vivi and the other waiters
      clean up the table.

                                              (CONTINUED)

66 CONTINUED: 66

Sylvia and Laura supervise the action from the front desk.

                    SYLVIA
          Well, the senator seemed pleased.

                    LAURA
          I'll say. He left a five hundred
          dollar tip. This guy wants us to
          vote for him next election.

Both smile. The young man of the day before arrives in his
motorcycle and parks it in front of the restaurant.

                    SYLVIA
          See you tomorrow.

Laura doesn't seems to understand.

                    LAURA
          Why?

With her chin, Sylvia points through the window at the young
man who takes off his helmet.

                    LAURA (CONT'D)
          Gosh girl, you're unbelievable.

                    SYLVIA
          No, I'm not.

The young man gets off the motorcycle. Laura elbows Sylvia
discreetly.

                    LAURA
          That's what I would like to have for
          Christmas. Have that in mind, ok?

67 EXT. WILLY'S -- DAY   67

Sylvia walks out. John comes out of the restaurant and faces
her.

                    JOHN
          Who the hell is this?

Sylvia stares at him without losing her cool.

                    SYLVIA
          A friend.

                                                        (CONTINUED)

67   CONTINUED: 67

                              JOHN
                    No, he's a customer. I saw him having
                    lunch here.

                              SYLVIA
                    He's a friend that ate lunch here
                    yesterday.

Sylvia turns around to get on the motorcycle. Her coldness
infuriates him. He takes two steps forward and faces Sylvia.

                              JOHN
                    So, you fuck whoever you wanna fuck?

Some of the waiters walk by and stare. Sylvia draws close to
John and mutters quietly to him.

                              SYLVIA
                    When you leave your wife, then you
                    can talk.

Sylvia gets on the bike.

                              SYLVIA (CONT'D)
                    Let's go.

She puts on her helmet. They ride off leaving John alone in
the parking lot.

68   EXT. HIGHWAY -- DAY   68

The young man rides his motorcycle down the curves of the
Pacific Highway. The sea shimmers in the sunset. Suddenly
from behind a Chevrolet Pick up truck pulls up next to them.

69   OMITTED   69

70   INT. TRUCK -- DAY   70

John is at the wheel. He opens the passenger`s window.

                              JOHN
                    Sylvia... Sylvia...

They can't hear with the helmets on. John honks repeatedly.

                              JOHN (CONT'D)
                    Where are you going Sylvia?

71   EXT. HIGHWAY -- DAY   71

The truck drives alongside them for a while. Suddenly in a
curve, a car appears in the opposite lane. Trying to avoid
it, John cuts in front of the motorcycle. The young man
loses control of the bike and it skids into the muddy side
of the road: a stupid accident.

John pulls over and scared, runs over to see what happened.
He sees the young man sitting up painfully and finds Sylvia
in the mud with a bloody nose. John approaches them
cautiously.

                    JOHN
          Are you ok?

Sylvia gets up.

                    SYLVIA
          You idiot.

                    JOHN
          I'm sorry. I didn't mean for this to
          happen.

                    SYLVIA
          Shut up.

The young man confronts John.

                    YOUNG MAN
          Are you stupid or what?

                    JOHN
          I'm sorry.

The young man pushes John out of his way to pick up his bike.
John pushes him back.

                    JOHN (CONT'D)
          Fuck you.

                    YOUNG MAN
          Fuck you.

Suddenly a modest Ikon pulls over on the side of the road.
Carlos gets out and sees the commotion.

Sylvia looks at the blood on her hands and the mud on her
dress. The young man picks up his bike and turns to her.

                              (CONTINUED)

                    YOUNG MAN (CONT'D)
          You sort your shit out with your
          boyfriend.

Without another word, he starts the engine and goes.   Sylvia
turns to John.

                    SYLVIA
          Get out of here.

                    JOHN
          Are you ok?

                    SYLVIA
          I said leave, goddamit.

She grabs a fistful of mud and throws it at him.   She begins
walking in the opposite direction, towards Carlos.   John
follows her.   She turns and shout at him.

                    SYLVIA (CONT'D)
          Go...

She continues walking.   Carlos approaches her.

                    CARLOS
          ¿Estás bien?
              (Are you alright?)

Sylvia pays no attention, worried about the bleeding.

                    SYLVIA
          I don't speak spanish.

John stops in his tracks.   Sylvia brings his hand to her
nose: the blood will not stop flowing. Carlos takes out a
handkerchief and hands it to her.

                    CARLOS
          No creo que esté rota.   [I don`t
          think you broke your nose.]

Sylvia takes the handkerchief and begins to clean her face.

                    CARLOS (CONT'D)
          Te llevo a tu casa, ¿si quieres?
              (I can drive you home
               if you want?)

Sylvia doesn't understand.

71   CONTINUED: (2)   71

                         SYLVIA
                 What do you want?

Carlos points at his car and mimes driving.

                         CARLOS
                 Llevarte a tu casa.
                     (To take you home.)

Sylvia turns to John and challenging him, she nods to Carlos.

                         SYLVIA
                 Ok.

                         JOHN
                 Sylvia, where are you going?

She stares at him and then goes inside the car.

72   INT. CARLOS CAR -- DAY   72

Carlos`s car winds down the highway by the ocean. Sylvia
takes off the handkerchief and sees she is no longer bleeding.

                         SYLVIA
                 That's better won't you say?

Carlos just smiles in response. She looks at him.

                         SYLVIA (CONT'D)
                 Whats your name?

                         CARLOS
                 Name? Yo...Carlos ¿y tú?
                     (My name? Carlos,
                      you?)

                         SYLVIA
                 Sylvia.

                         CARLOS
                 ¿Sylvia?

                         SYLVIA
                 Yeah, Sylvia.

Carlos gazes at her curiously.

72A   OMITTED   72A

73   EXT. STREET, SYLVIA'S APARTMENT -- DAY   73

The Ikon pulls up outside Sylvia's apartment building.

74   INT. CARLOS'S CAR -- AFTERNOON   74

Sylvia looks toward her house.

                    SYLVIA
                (In broken Spanish)
           Gracias. [Thanks.]

                    CARLOS
           De nada. [You're welcome.]

Sylvia points at the apartment.

                    SYLVIA
           D'you wanna come in?

Carlos doesn't understand. Sylvia points at the apartment,
then at him.

                    SYLVIA (CONT'D)
           Come in...you....

Carlos seems to get it.

                    CARLOS
           Come in?

                    SYLVIA
           Yes...come in...

He thinks for a moment, then nods.

75   INT. SYLVIA'S HOUSE -- DAY   75

Sylvia opens the door and Carlos walks in somewhat shyly.

                    SYLVIA
           Do you want something to drink?

                    CARLOS
           ¿Drink? No drink, gracias. [Drink?
           No drink, thank you.]

She goes to look at herself in the mirror: she examines her
nose and then sees her stained dress. She turns to Carlos.

                    SYLVIA
           That was my favorite dress.

(CONTINUED)

CONTINUED:

Without another word she takes it off and is left wearing
only her panties. She puts on a robe but leaves it untied.
Carlos holds his breath. She acts naturally.

> SYLVIA (CONT'D)
> I hope the blood comes out in the
> wash.

She throws it into the sink and walks over to Carlos. She
leans in to kiss him, but he pulls away. She smiles and tries
to kiss him again. He moves again.

> CARLOS
> No.

Sylvia is surprised: she's not used to being rejected. She
opens the robe seductively.

> SYLVIA
> Don't you like me?

She smiles and tries again. Carlos now decisively stops her
by holding her shoulders.

> CARLOS
> No.

She is confused. Carlos steps back and stares at her. He
reaches out and with the back of his index finger he softly
strokes her nipple. She looks at him even more surprised.

Suddenly, Carlos pulls his hand away, turns on his heel and
leaves the house. Sylvia is left standing there.

76   EXT. MAROMA CEMETERY -- DAY   76

A large group of mourners accompanies Gina's family. Robert
is torn apart, weeping. His children cry quietly, except for
Mariana, who watches the coffin descend with a hard, mute
expression on her face. Hidden under the shadow of a mesquite
is the Martinez pickup truck.

77   INT. PICKUP TRUCK -- DAY   77

Santiago spies the funeral, and, specifically, Mariana.

78   EXT. MAROMA CEMETERY -- DAY   78

The mourners file out of the cemetery and get into their
cars. Santiago ducks so as not to be seen. Further off,
Mariana, her siblings and her father get into a Ford 1980
ten-seater van and leave.

79   INT. PICKUP TRUCK -- DAY   79

Santiago starts the truck and follows them.

80   EXT. STREET, TOWN -- DAY   80

The Van drives down some dusty streets until it stops in
front of Gina's house.

81   INT. PICKUP TRUCK -- DAY   81

Santiago parks at a safe distance and watches how Mariana
and the rest of the family enter the house.

82   EXT. STREET, TOWN -- DAY   82

The sun shines brightly on the dusty streets.

83   INT. PICKUP TRUCK -- DAY   83

Santiago sits in the truck listening to Mexican songs on the
radio while he watches Gina's house.

84   EXT. GINA'S HOUSE -- DAY   84

Mariana steps out of the house and starts to walk down the
street in the opposite direction.

85   INT. PICKUP TRUCK -- DAY   85

Santiago watches Mariana. He makes sure no one is watching
him, and discreetly gets out of the truck and follows her.

86   EXT. STREET, TOWN -- DAY   86

Mariana walks five blocks until she enters a small grocery
store. Santiago follows her at a distance.

87   INT. GROCERY STORE -- DAY   87

Santiago spots Mariana in the back, taking some quarts of
milk out of the refrigerator. Santiago walks up to her. She
feels his presence and turns around. She stares at him.

                         SANTIAGO
              Do you know who I am?

Mariana nods. They are quiet for a moment.

                    SANTIAGO (CONT'D)
              I'm not here to fight.

                                              (CONTINUED)

87   CONTINUED: 87

>   MARIANA
>   Then what do you want?
>
>   SANTIAGO
>   I want to know more. That's all. Who
>   your mom was, what she did with my
>   dad.
>
>   MARIANA
>   We already know what she did.
>
>   SANTIAGO
>   No, we don't.

Again, they are silent.

>   SANTIAGO (CONT'D)
>   Can I talk to you some day?

She nods.

>   SANTIAGO (CONT'D)
>   Ok. I'll come look for you.

88   EXT. SORGHUM FIELDS, TAMAULIPAS -- DAY   88

The crop duster passes flying low over the sorghum and then
pulls up again. A jackrabbit shoots out of the field,
frightened by the plane, and zig-zags away for cover.

89   EXT. SHACK -- DAY   89

Maria cooks in the shack. Through the windows we can see the
plane spraying, turning, flying low.

We hear the plane making a strange noise. Maria turns toward
the window. The plane is diving, but does not seem like it
is going to pull up. Maria watches, frozen.

Suddenly, the plane crashes loudly into the sorghum fields,
lifting up a dust cloud. We hear the shattering of glass,
the rending of metal. Maria stands stupefied, then runs out.

90   EXT. SORGHUM FIELDS, TAMAULIPAS -- DAY   90

Maria runs through the fields. Further off, we see the crop
duster destroyed, smoke burgeoning out of one of its wings.
Maria runs anxiously up to the scene of the accident.

>   MARIA
>   Daddy... daddy...

91   INT. CROP DUSTER -- DAY   91

Santiago sits with his face covered in blood. He can barely
move. Two lengths of twisted metal are sticking into his
left thigh. The raw muscle is bleeding through his torn pants.

92   EXT. SCENE OF THE CRASH -- CONTINUOUS   92

Maria climbs onto the wreck.

>   MARIA
>   Daddy... daddy...

>   SANTIAGO
>   I'm fine sweetie... don't worry...

She struggles to climb into the cockpit.

>   SANTIAGO (CONT'D)
>   Sweetie... be calm...

She hugs him, crying. Santiago grabs the radio and tries to
call, but it is broken.

She uncovers the leg perforated by the shattered metal, and
reveals the deep wound from which blood oozes thickly.

She tries to pull the metal out, but it is impossible. She
tries again and hurts her hand.

>   SANTIAGO (CONT'D)
>   Sweetie, try to find something to
>   make a tourniquet.

She rummages inside the plane and finds a rag between the
seats. Maria cleans the blood off her father and makes a
tourniquet.

>   MARIA
>   Is that ok?

Santiago nods and strokes her hair.

>   SANTIAGO
>   Now you need to get help.

>   MARIA
>   I'm not leaving you.

>   SANTIAGO
>   Maria: you need to get help.

                                              (CONTINUED)

92   CONTINUED: 92

Maria looks at him, assents and runs off.

93   EXT. SORGHUM FIELDS, TAMAULIPAS -- DAY   93

Maria runs through the fields, screaming.

                        MARIA
            Auxilio...auxilio... [Help...help...]

No one is there. Only the stalks of orange sorghum and white
winged doves flying overhead.

She stops to gather her breath. She is sweating. The cicadas
grate and whir. She turns toward the plane.

She has left it far behind, wrecked, with her father dying
inside it.

She starts to run again, anxious, pouring sweat and panting.

                    MARIA (CONT'D)
            Auxilio...auxilio... [Help...help...]

Far away she spots Carlos on his bike, approaching.
Determined, she starts to race desperately toward him.

                    MARIA (CONT'D)
            Carlos...Carlos...

93A   EXT. PATH -- DAY   93A

Carlos hears Maria's distant shouts, and sees her diminutive
figure running towards him. He pedals hurriedly toward her.

93B   OMITTED   93B

94   EXT. GINA'S HOUSE -- MORNING   94

Gina is feeding maize to some chickens. They hurry to snatch
the grains away from each other.

An enormous trailer parks in front of the house. The door
opens and Robert hops out dressed in jeans, a white t-shirt
and a John Deere cap.

He opens the door to the patio, walks in and approaches Gina.

                        ROBERT
            Hey darlin'.

He gives her a kiss on the cheek.

                                                        (CONTINUED)

94   CONTINUED: 94

                         GINA
              Hi... I thought you didn't get back
              till tomorrow.

                         ROBERT
              Yeah, but I wrapped up early. Where
              are the kids?

                         GINA
              They went to a baseball game.
                   (a beat)
              You wanna wait on them for lunch?

Robert nods.

95   EXT. PATIO, GINA'S HOUSE -- DAY   95

Robert is kneeling in front of the grill fixing the gas pipe
that runs from the propane gas tank to the burners. Gina
comes out of the kitchen with a beer and hands it to him.
Robert takes it.

                         ROBERT
              Thanks.

He gives a sip and continues his work.

                         ROBERT (CONT'D)
              I will have this working again.

                         GINA
              We haven't used it in a while.

                         ROBERT
              There will be time.

Gina stays there a moment looking at him.

                         GINA
              I have to go out in the evenin'.

                         ROBERT
              Where?

                         GINA
              The Santa Elena K-Mart.

Robert stands up and goes to the patio table. He rummages
inside a box of tools and picks up a screwdriver.

                         ROBERT
              I'll come with you.

                              (CONTINUED)

He kneels again at the gas tank.

>   GINA
>   But then I've got to go buy some
>   fabric and then go to the butcher's.

>   ROBERT
>   Doesn't matter, I'll ride along. I
>   need to get me a radio.

Robert stands up and takes a lighter. Gina remains silent.
Robert tries to light the burners. He can't. He turns the
gas tank valve once and again and keeps trying.

Her four kids come down the street. When they are getting in
Robert tries once more to light the burners and a huge blaze
arises in the grill.

Robert steps back. Gina and the kids turn to him, scared.

>   GINA
>   Are you alright?

Robert smiles.

>   ROBERT
>   Of course I'm right.

Robert lights again the burners and now they work well.

>   ROBERT (CONT'D)
>   Now it works.

Monnie runs to her daddy.

>   MONNIE
>   Daddy, daddy...you scared me.

She hugs and kisses him. Mariana walks to her father.

>   MARIANA
>   Hi daddy.

Robert stands up and hugs his eldest daughter.

>   ROBERT
>   Hey little girl.

Mariana kisses him on the cheek. She turns to her mother.

95   CONTINUED: (2)   95

                          MARIANA
                     (gesturing at her
                     siblings)
                  D'you want me to fix them some lunch?

                          GINA
                  Set the table baby. I'll be right
                  in.

96   INT. KITCHEN, GINA'S HOUSE -- DAY   96

        Mariana ladles soup into some bowls while her siblings wait
        at the table. Bobby starts to eat in a hurry. Robert and
        Gina walk in. Robert stares at his son in disapproval.

                          ROBERT
                  Aren't you forgettin' something?

        Bobby looks at his father, afraid.

                          BOBBY
                  Sorry...

        He lowers his head and holds out his hands for his siblings.
        Mariana finishes serving, sits down and holds Monnie and
        Bobby's hands.

                          MARIANA
                  We thank you oh Lord for our daily
                  bread, and for the love and happiness
                  you bestow upon this home.

        They let go of each other and get ready to eat.

                          ROBERT
                  Bobby, let that be the last time you
                  offend our Lord.

                          BOBBY
                  Yes sir.

        Mariana and her mother exchange glances. Robert smiles and
        leans on the sink.

                          ROBERT
                     (to the kids)
                  Hey, me and your mom are goin' to
                  Santa Elena. You wanna come?

                          BOBBY AND MONNIE
                  Yeah!

(CONTINUED)

96   CONTINUED: 96

Gina quickly interrupts.

                    GINA
          But the kids have homework to do.

                    ROBERT
          We'll go and come back in a flash.

                    BOBBY AND MONNIE
          Yeah, come on, please...

Gina sighs, disappointed.

97   EXT. GINA'S HOUSE -- DAY   97

The children and Robert are getting into the van. Gina doesn't
get in and stands in front of the passenger door.

                    GINA
          Damn, I forgot my wallet.

She goes back in. Then, Mariana decides to also go back in.

                    MARIANA
          Then I'm gonna go pee.

98   INT. HALLWAY, GINA'S HOUSE -- DAY   98

Gina is on the phone. She looks nervous.

                    GINA
          Nick, I don't think I can see you...
          Robert said he'd come with me and
          he's bringin' the kids... I'm miss
          you too... I'll try to get loose...I
          love you...bye.

She hangs up and sees Robert and the kids in the van. She
turns around and encounters Mariana, at the end of the
hallway, watching her. Gina gets flustered.

                    MARIANA
          Who were you talking to?

                    GINA
              (trying to regain her
              composure)
          Your aunt Leticia...

Mariana looks her straight in the eye. Gina signals the van.

                                              (CONTINUED)

98   CONTINUED: 98

> GINA (CONT'D)
> Come on now, they're waitin' for us.

Mariana walks away toward the rooms.

> GINA (CONT'D)
> Where are you going?

> MARIANA
> Bathroom.

99   INT. WAL-MART -- DAY   99

The family enters the Wal-Mart. Monnie stops in front of some dolls.

> MONNIE
> Daddy, I want that one...

> ROBERT
> No baby, we have to save up now...

Gina turns to Mariana and hands her a list.

> GINA
> I need you to get these and please
> help Monnie pick out a blouse.
> (to Robert)
> Can you give me the keys to the van,
> I'm gonna go get the fabric I ordered.

Mariana looks at her mistrustfully.

> MONNIE
> I wanna come with you...

> GINA
> No. Go with your sister and pick out
> a blouse. I won't be long.

Robert hands her the keys to the van. Gina takes the keys and turns to leave. She walks toward the exit breathing through her mouth.

100   INT. VAN -- DAY   100

Gina shuts the door and, nervous, leans on the steering wheel.

101   EXT. PARKING LOT -- DAY   101

Mariana walks out into the parking lot just in time to see her mother make a right and drive off toward the town.

102   INT. VAN -- DAY   102

Gina drives down a dirt road. Further off she spots Nick's
truck. He is sitting on the hood.

103   EXT. PATH -- DAY   103

Upon seeing her arrive, Nick slides off the hood to greet
her. She parks and gets out.

She starts to kiss him as soon as she sees him.

                    GINA
          I missed you... I missed you...

They kiss for a long time.

104   EXT. WAL-MART -- DAY   104

Robert and the kids are outside, waiting with their shopping
carts full of the things they bought.

                    PAT
          Mom's takin' a long time.

                    ROBERT
          She had stuff to do.

Mariana looks at both of them and then at the parking lot.
In the distance we can see the van arrive.

                    ROBERT (CONT'D)
          There she is.

Gina pulls up in front of them and gets out.

                    GINA
          I'm sorry, but they didn't have my
          order ready and they made me wait.
          I have to come back to pick it up,
          or I won't be able to make Monnie's
          dress for her school presentation.

She talks quickly and clumsily. Robert points at the trunk.

                    ROBERT
          Can you open the trunk?

                    GINA
          Oh sure, sure...

                                              (CONTINUED)

104   CONTINUED: 104

Gina turns around to open. The others wheel their shopping
carts to the back of the van and start unloading. Gina helps.

                    GINA (CONT'D)
                 (to Mariana)
            Did you get everything on the list?

Mariana just stares at her. She turns around and gets into
the van. Gina, disconcerted, watches her go. Robert snaps
her out of it when he moves her aside to close the trunk.

105   OMITTED   105

106   EXT. RIVERSIDE ROAD -- DAY   106

Sylvia is walking in the park that runs along the river.

She feels someone there and turns. Carlos is watching her
some twenty yards away. She looks at him for a moment. Carlos
slowly walks over until he is close to her.

                    SYLVIA
            What are you doing?...What do you
            want?

Carlos looks uncomfortable. He gazes out at the river, as if
there he might find the right words.

                    CARLOS
            Tenemos que hablar Mariana. [We
            need to talk Mariana.]

Upon hearing her name, Sylvia freezes.

                    SYLVIA
            You have the wrong girl, my name is
            Sylvia ok?

She walks around him and tries to leave. Carlos cuts her
off.

                    CARLOS
            Santiago me mandó a buscarte.
            [Santiago sent me to look for you.]

On hearing Santiago's name, Sylvia looks disturbed: it weighs
on her.

                    SYLVIA
            What did you just say?

106   CONTINUED: 106

                         CARLOS
          Santiago... me mandó a buscarte.

From his shirt pocket, Carlos takes out a photograph and
hands it to her.

                   CARLOS (CONT'D)
          Mariana, esta es tu hija, se llama
          María. [This is your daughter, her
          name is Maria.]

Sylvia looks at the picture, notably shocked, and then gives
it back to him.

                   SYLVIA
          Stay away from me.

Without saying anything else, Sylvia leaves. Carlos watches
her go.

107   INT. SANTIAGO'S HOUSE -- MORNING   107

Santiago is sleeping in his bed. He hears some noise outside.
He opens the drapes and through the window he sees a pick up
truck parked in front of the house. Cristobal and a young
man are carrying some men's clothes into the truck under the
supervision of a priest (45).

Hurriedly, Santiago puts on some pants and a shirt and runs
out.

107A   EXT. SANTIAGO'S HOUSE -- MORNING   107A

Santiago gets out of the house and goes directly to the truck.
He points the clothes to his brother.

                   SANTIAGO
          Those are my father's clothes.

                   CRISTOBAL
          Mom wants to get rid of them.

The young man lands a box on the cargo box.

                   SANTIAGO
          We can't throw them away.

                   PRIEST
          You're not throwing anything away,
          these are for the homeless. It's a
          good thing my son.

(CONTINUED)

Santiago turns to the priest.

> SANTIAGO
> I'm sorry father, we're going to
> take them back.

He begins putting the clothes back in the box. While he is doing so, Ana goes out and stands on the porch.

> ANA
> Santiago. What are you doing?

Santiago takes one of the shirts and shows it to his mother.

> SANTIAGO
> These were my dad's favorite shirts.

Ana walks to them.

> ANA
> So?

> SANTIAGO
> My father wore them, he worked in
> them, he played with us in them.

> ANA
> Put them back in the truck.

The priest intervenes to soften the imminent confrontation.

> PRIEST
> Santiago. It's a good thing to give
> them away. It's good for you, your
> brother and your mother. It's better
> to begin a new life.

> SANTIAGO
> A new life?

Santiago grabs a bunch of his father's clothes and heads back to his house.

> ANA
> Santiago, bring them back. Santiago.

Santiago doesn't turns back. He goes into the house and closes the door.

108   INT. TRUCK -- DAY   108

Santiago sits in the truck, waiting. The temperature hovers
around 110 degrees, and he sweats profusely.

He carefully watches Gina's house. He sees Robert and Pat
walk out, get into the van and leave.

109   EXT. GINA'S HOUSE -- DAY   109

Santiago carefully opens the gate and enters the garden.

Santiago walks around and examines the place, room by room,
through the windows. He walks over to the main bedroom, which
is empty. On the wall is a large photograph of Gina and Robert
(20 and 22 respectively) on the day of their wedding.

Santiago scans Gina's face, her hands, her hair. He then
keeps walking until he reaches Mariana's room. She is lying
on her back, staring at the ceiling.

Santiago knocks on the window.

110   INT. MARIANA'S ROOM -- DAY   110

At first, Mariana can't tell where the noise is coming from,
until she turns and encounters Santiago's penetrating gaze.

She gets up and opens the window.

                    MARIANA
          What are you doing? If my dad finds
          out you're here he's gonna kill you.

                    SANTIAGO
          I told you I'd come look for you.

                    MARIANA
          Yeah, but not here.
               (a beat)
          Wait for me at the windmill, on the
          way to Guadalupe.

                    SANTIAGO
          Ok.

Santiago leaves and Mariana closes the window.

111   EXT. WINDMILL -- DAY   111

The pickup truck is parked under a cluster of mesquites.
Santiago is leaning on a truck with a slingshot in his hand.

                                              (CONTINUED)

111   CONTINUED: 111

A white winged dove alights on the top of the tree and
Santiago shoots at it. He misses.

Mariana arrives on a bike. She dismounts and walks toward
Santiago, who puts the slingshot in his back pocket.

                    MARIANA
          Why d'you want to see me?

Santiago shrugs his shoulders.

                    SANTIAGO
          I dunno.

                    MARIANA
          I don't think it's ok for you to
          talk to me.

                    SANTIAGO
          Why?

Mariana doesn't answer. Some quails run along the path.
Santiago pulls out his slingshot, picks up a stone and fires
without hitting them. The covey takes flight.

They are silent. They look uncomfortable.

                    SANTIAGO (CONT'D)
          Do you look like your mom?

                    MARIANA
          No. Do you look like your dad?

                    SANTIAGO
          A little.
               (a beat)
          Do you know how your mom and my dad
          met?

                    MARIANA
          No. I have no idea.

A quail that was left behind appears on the path. Mariana
points at Santiago's slingshot.

                    MARIANA (CONT'D)
               (quietly)
          Hand it over.

Santiago hands it over. Mariana picks up a stone. She shoots
and hits. Mariana turns and looks at him, overjoyed.

                                          (CONTINUED)

111   CONTINUED: (2)   111

                    MARIANA (CONT'D)
          I got it.

They walk over to it and find the quail on its last legs.
Mariana picks it up and shows it to him.

                    MARIANA (CONT'D)
          Let's eat it.

112   EXT. NEW MEXICO DESERT -- DAY   112

Mariana and Santiago are sitting around a small fire. The
quail is roasting on a stone slab.

                    SANTIAGO
          Do you like hunting?

                    MARIANA
          A lot. A boyfriend used to take me,
          but I haven't gone back since we
          broke up.

                    SANTIAGO
          My dad taught me to hunt.

They are quiet for a moment. The fire sputters.

                    MARIANA
          Did you love your dad?

Santiago nods.

                    MARIANA (CONT'D)
          I loved my mom too, but I didn't
          like her.
               (a beat)
          D'you have any pictures?

Santiago pulls out his old, worn wallet, and rummages among
the pockets until he takes out a black and white photograph
of Nick, - the kind taken at a photo booth.

He shows it to Mariana, who looks at it disdainfully.

                    MARIANA (CONT'D)
          You don't look like him at all.

Mariana hands it back and points at the quail.

                    MARIANA (CONT'D)
          It's done, take it off.

                                                    (CONTINUED)

112   CONTINUED: 112

Santiago tries to get the quail out with a stick, but the
flames make him pull his arm back.

                         SANTIAGO
              I can't, it's too hot.

Mariana looks at him, and then, undaunted, grabs the quail,
pulls it out, and holds it on the palm of her hand.

                         SANTIAGO (CONT'D)
              Doesn't it burn?

                         MARIANA
              Yeah, but I can control the pain.

Mariana grabs the quail with her other hand, splits it down
the middle and hands Santiago his half, who juggles with it
to avoid getting burned. Mariana starts to eat her half.

113   EXT. DESERT PATH -- DAY   113

The sun drops below the horizon. Santiago's truck drives
down a desert road and stops near the cluster of houses.

Mariana steps out of the truck, and gets her bike from the
back. She hops on and as she passes Santiago he leans out
the window.

                         SANTIAGO
              I'll come get you tomorrow. Bring
              pictures of your mom.

Mariana stops to listen to him and then rides on.

113A   OMITTED   113A

114   INT. HOSPITAL WAITING ROOM -- NIGHT   114

Carlos and Maria sit in a small waiting room. Carlos points
at a soda vending machine.

                         CARLOS
              ¿Quieres una Coca? [D'you want a
              coke?]

Maria nods. Her eyes are swollen from crying and she is filthy
with dust and blood. Carlos puts some coins in the machine
and takes out two cans. He opens one and gives it to Maria.

                         MARIA
              Gracias... [Thanks...]

                                                    (CONTINUED)

114   CONTINUED: 114

          She starts to drink. A doctor walks up to them.

                              DOCTOR
                    ¿Es usted Carlos Alarid? [Are you
                    Carlos Alarid?]

                              CARLOS
                    Sí, yo soy. [Yes, I am.]

                              DOCTOR
                    El paciente pidió hablar con usted.
                    [The patient asked to talk to you.]

          Maria gets up, but the doctor stops her.

                              DOCTOR (CONT'D)
                    Pidió hablar sólo con él. [He asked
                    to speak to him alone.]

          Carlos caresses her head to calm her down.

                              CARLOS
                    Ahorita vengo por ti. [I'll be right
                    back.]

          He heads toward the room.

115   INT. HALLWAY, HOSPITAL -- NIGHT   115

          Carlos and Santiago talk for a long time in the room, while
          Maria watches them from the hall. After a while, Carlos looks
          out and calls her in.

                              CARLOS
                    Maria, ven. [Come in, Maria.]

116   INT. HOSPITAL ROOM -- NIGHT   116

          Maria walks in quietly. She is stunned to see her father
          hooked up. Carlos moves aside.

                              SANTIAGO
                    Maria, I want you to listen to Carlos.
                    I want you to do whatever he says.

                              MARIA
                    Are you going to be ok?

                              SANTIAGO
                    Yeah, I'm going to be fine. But
                    promise me you'll do whatever Carlos
                    tells you.

                                                      (CONTINUED)

116   CONTINUED: 116

                          MARIA
                You promise you'll be ok?

Santiago thinks about his answer for a moment.

                          SANTIAGO
                I promise. Do you?

Maria thinks for a second, then nods.

                          SANTIAGO (CONT'D)
                Just do whatever Carlos tells you to
                do, ok?

117   EXT. TRAILER HOME -- DAY   117

Nick arrives in his truck and parks. Gina's Ford Pinto is
parked outside the trailer. Nick gets out of the truck, opens
the door to the trailer home and walks in.

118   INT. TRAILER HOME -- DAY   118

The place looks neat and clean. Nick sees Gina washing dishes
in the sink. She turns to look at him.

                          GINA
                Hi.

Nick looks around, amazed.

                          NICK
                Wow, look at this place!

Nick walks up to her and kisses her neck. She writhes.

                          GINA
                It's been a month, today.

                          NICK
                So, are you happy?

                          GINA
                Very, but I'd be even happier if we
                had some hot water. I couldn't shower.

Nick starts to lick her.

                          NICK
                You're tastier this way.

Nick keeps licking her. He tries to put his hand under her
blouse, to touch her breasts, but she stops him.

                                            (CONTINUED)

118   CONTINUED: 118

                              GINA
                    Not there. Please.

Nick pulls back and looks at her.

                              NICK
                    Why?

                              GINA
                    I don't like that part of my body.

                              NICK
                    How d'you know I'm not gonna like
                    it?

Gina remains quiet, pensive.

                              GINA
                    I don't want you to leave me.

                              NICK
                    And I don't wanna leave you.

Again, Gina is silent. She slowly starts to unbutton her
blouse. She opens it and unsnaps her bra. In place of her
right breast is a long scar.

                              GINA
                    I had cancer two years ago.

Nick draws close to her. He opens her blouse even wider,
kneels down and softly kisses her scar. She hugs him tightly
as she starts to cry softly.

119   INT. LIVING ROOM, GINA'S HOUSE -- NIGHT   119

All the lights are off. Gina walks in and silently closes
the door.

120   INT. HALLWAY, GINA'S HOUSE -- NIGHT   120

She quietly peers into her boys' room: they are asleep. She
then looks into Mariana and Monnie's room. Monnie is asleep,
and Mariana is reading in bed.

                              MARIANA
                    Where were you?

                              GINA
                    I was at Libby's.

Mariana looks at her skeptically.

                                                      (CONTINUED)

120   CONTINUED: 120

                          MARIANA
                Bobby cut his arm with a piece of
                glass and Dr. Page had to sew him
                up.

                          GINA
                Is he ok?

                          MARIANA
                Yeah, he's fine.

Gina turns around and goes into the boys room. Mariana
follows.

120A   OMITTED   120A

120B   INT. BOYS ROOM -- NIGHT   120B

She gets in, turns on the table lamp and sits on Bobby's
bed. She takes his arm and examines the wound. It has a large
stitch running through his right forearm. Bobby remains
asleep.

Mariana stands behind her.

                          MARIA
                He wouldn't stop crying and asking
                for you.

Gina turns to see Mariana.

                          MARIANA
                Good night, mom.

She leaves the room. Gina stays there, pensive.

121   EXT. GINA'S HOUSE -- DAY   121

Mariana and her siblings leave with their backpacks on.
Gina waves goodbye from the door.

                          GINA
                Y'all be good, now.

She walks in and closes the door.

122   EXT. STREET, TOWN -- DAY   122

The four are walking away when Mariana stops.

                                              (CONTINUED)

122   CONTINUED: 122

> MARIANA
> I forgot my homework. Keep goin' and
> I'll catch up with you later.

> PAT
> We'll wait for you.

> MARIANA
> No, go on.

They part. Mariana watches them disappear among the streets.
She walks back home.

123   EXT. GINA'S HOUSE -- DAY   123

She carefully opens the gate. She goes to get her bicycle,
which is leaning on the porch. She gets on, rides out of the
house and pedals toward the town exit.

124   EXT. CLUSTER OF TREES -- DAY   124

Mariana hides behind some trees, spying out the highway.
The heat makes her sweat. She hears the sound of white wing
doves flying overhead.

In the distance, a car is approaching: her mother's Pinto,
which soon enough drives past. Mariana jumps on her bike and
starts to follow it, pedaling as fast as she can.

125   EXT. PATH -- DAY   125

Just when it seems as if Mariana is going to lose the Pinto,
it turns onto a path.

Mariana follows her up to the turn off. She stops to look.
The Pinto is hard to miss: it kicks up a huge dust cloud
that Mariana decides to follow.

126   EXT. TRAILER HOME -- DAY   126

Gina reaches the trailer home and parks. Nick's truck is
already there. She hears noises from behind the house and
goes to see. It is Nick, trying to hook up a gas tank.

Upon seeing her, Nick smiles.

> NICK
> Now we're gonna finally get us some
> hot water.

She hugs him from behind and kisses the back of his neck.

126   CONTINUED: 126

> NICK (CONT'D)
> Come on, let's take a shower.

Gina looks pensive.

> GINA
> I don't know if I can.

> NICK
> Yes, you can, come on.

Nick lifts Gina up and carries her indoors.

127   EXT. NEW MEXICO DESERT -- DAY   127

From a cluster of mesquites, Mariana watches her mother kissing and hugging the unknown man. She breathes agitatedly, her eyes nailed to the couple.

128   INT. SHOWER -- DAY   128

Nick and Gina are under the shower, kissing. Nick caresses her whole body: her buttocks, her belly, her back. She holds him tightly. Naked, she looks more fragile than ever: a little bird between his arms.

128A   EXT. TRAILER HOME -- DAY   128A

Mariana is spying on them through the window. The bathroom door is open. Through the transparent shower curtain, she can see the naked bodies hugging. Horrified, she looks down.

128B   OMITTED   128B

129   INT. SYLVIA'S HOUSE -- NIGHT   129

Sylvia is sitting at the table. On the table are old and worn out pictures of a newborn baby. She stares at them for a while.

Sylvia lets her head drop back, her eyes full of tears.

130   INT. WILLY'S -- DAY   130

The restaurant is bustling. Sylvia, pale and exhausted, works mechanically, lost in her thoughts. Sophie approaches her.

> SOPHIE
> Sylvia, Mr. Jordan called, he is
> bringing a big party of eight and we
> are booked...

130   CONTINUED: 130

Sylvia looks at her, dazed.

                    SYLVIA
          I know, but what do you want me to
          do Sophie?

Sylvia looks on distantly at the customers.

                    SOPHIE
          Are you ok?

                    SYLVIA
          Just take care of things for a while,
          I will be back.

131   INT. KITCHEN, RESTAURANT -- DAY   131

John is concentrating on dicing some vegetables on a chopping
board. Sylvia walks up to him. John is surprised to see
her.

                    JOHN
          Hi.

                    SYLVIA
          Come outside. We need to talk.

132   EXT. WILLY'S -- DAY   132

They walk out the back door and stand beside the dumpsters.

                    JOHN
          What's up?

                    SYLVIA
          Do you like me?

John nods. Sylvia looks anxious; her eyes dart all over the
place.

                    SYLVIA (CONT'D)
          I mean do you think you could love
          me?

The question catches John off guard.

                    JOHN
          I don`t know... I guess so.

                    SYLVIA
          Let's just get out of here...just me
          and you, today.

                                              (CONTINUED)

132   CONTINUED: 132

                          JOHN
              What are you talking about?

                          SYLVIA
              Just pack your car and go somewhere
              new and start over, somewhere newer
              than here...just let's go.

                          JOHN
              I don't understand.

                          SYLVIA
              Yes or no?

                          JOHN
              I don't know, I have to think about
              it.

     Sylvia frustrated, turns and walks back into the restaurant.
     John is shaken by the whirlwind of Sylvia's proposition.

133   EXT. STREET, CITY -- DAY   133

     Laura's car parks in front of Sylvia's building. She gets
     out and waves goodbye. Laura drives off.

     Sylvia looks both ways and opens the door.

134   INT. STAIRS, SYLVIA'S HOUSE -- DAY   134

     She walks in and sees Carlos with Maria in the hall that
     leads up to her house. She turns her back to leave.

     Carlos notices her and begins to call her.

                          CARLOS
              Mariana, Mariana...

     Sylvia disappears around the corner.

135   EXT. CLUSTER OF TREES WINDMILL -- AFTERNOON   135

     Santiago and Mariana sit, looking at photographs. Santiago
     has a picture of Robert and Gina in the Grand Canyon.

                          MARIANA
              Here they are, at the Grand Canyon,
              on their honeymoon.

     Mariana hands him another photograph.

135   CONTINUED: 135

                        MARIANA (CONT'D)
                  That's my mom and dad with us when
                  we were little.

Santiago looks at her: Robert and Gina are surrounded by
their four children. He looks closely at Mariana's face in
the picture.

                        SANTIAGO
                  You look like Betty, from Archie.

Mariana gives him a little push. She shows him another one.

                        MARIANA
                  This is my mother's last picture.
                  It's her birthday.

Santiago takes it and looks at it for a long time: Gina is
smiling, holding Mariana.

Then Mariana gives him a photograph of herself.

                        MARIANA (CONT'D)
                  And this is me.

                        SANTIAGO
                  Can I have this one?

Mariana considers her answer.

                        MARIANA
                  Only if you give me a scar.

                        SANTIAGO
                  What?

                        MARIANA
                  I want a scar to remember this day.

                        SANTIAGO
                  Will you give me one?

They remain silent. Mariana puts the other photos away.

                        MARIANA
                  My dad's away on business. Come get
                  me tonight. Let's go to the desert
                  to burn chollas.

135A   OMITTED   135A

136   EXT. NEW MEXICO DESERT -- NIGHT   136

Mariana and Santiago stand before a cholla. Mariana sets
fire to it with a lighter. The cholla burns quickly, turning
the darkness orange together with both their faces. The fire
burns for less than a minute and the charred cholla collapses.

> MARIANA
> A cowboy told me that the smoke of a
> burnt cholla is purifying.

> SANTIAGO
> They burn like fireworks.

> MARIANA
> Yes, I love it.

She stares at him.

> MARIANA (CONT'D)
> (a beat)
> Roll up your sleeves.

> SANTIAGO
> What for?

> MARIANA
> So you can give me your scar.

Santiago rolls up his sleeves. Mariana flicks on the lighter
and sets the flame on his arm. Santiago holds for a while,
then pulls away.

> SANTIAGO
> Shit! That burns!

> MARIANA
> If you concentrate it doesn't hurt.

She lights the lighter and holds it under her forearm.
Santiago watches her fixedly. Several seconds go by and smoke
starts to come out of her skin.

> SANTIAGO
> Stop, you're going to hurt yourself.

Mariana remains impassive as the flame chars her forearm.

> SANTIAGO (CONT'D)
> Enough now, stop it.

Mariana shows him a large burn above her wrist.

(CONTINUED)

136   CONTINUED: 136

                              MARIANA
                    This scar's for you.

Santiago takes the lighter away from her, lights it and holds
his forearm over the flame. He stoically holds it as long
as he can. He is in tremendous pain, but doesn't pull away.

Smoke emerges. Tears roll out of Santiago's eyes, but Santiago
bears the pain. After a while he shows her his scar.

                              SANTIAGO
                    And this one's yours.

137   EXT. GINA'S HOUSE -- NIGHT   137

The truck parks behind the house.

138   INT. TRUCK -- NIGHT   138

                              MARIANA
                    Good night.

Mariana is about to get out. Santiago holds her elbow.

                              SANTIAGO
                    Let me sleep with you.

                              MARIANA
                    Are you crazy?

                              SANTIAGO
                    I swear I won't lay a finger on you.

Mariana thinks about it.

                              MARIANA
                    You're gonna wake up my sister Monnie.

                              SANTIAGO
                    Your dad's not home. We can sleep in
                    his room.

139   INT. ROOM, GINA'S HOUSE -- NIGHT   139

Mariana and Santiago enter the bedroom. She carefully closes
the door, walks over to a nightstand and turns on a bedside
lamp. Santiago, full of curiosity, examines the room.

                              SANTIAGO
                    What side did your mom sleep on?

                                                              (CONTINUED)

139   CONTINUED: 139

Mariana points at the right side. Santiago sits there and
looks over the items on the nightstand: a box of kleenex,
medicine, a glass.

                    SANTIAGO (CONT'D)
              What did your mom wear to bed?
              Pajamas? A slip?

                    MARIANA
              Why d'you wanna know?

                    SANTIAGO
              I want to know everything about her.

                    MARIANA
              A slip.

                    SANTIAGO
              Can you put it on? Please.

Mariana looks at him mistrustfully.

                    MARIANA
              It's not right to dress in the clothes
              of the dead.

                    SANTIAGO
              I'm wearing my dad's shirt.

Mariana considers.

                    MARIANA
              You promise not to touch me.

                    SANTIAGO
              I promise.

Mariana goes to a closet, takes out the slip and goes out
into the bathroom.

139A   INT. BATHROOM -- NIGHT   139A

Mariana gets into the bathroom. She examines the slip before
putting it. She begins to unbutton her blouse.

139B   INT. HALLWAY, GINA'S HOUSE -- NIGHT   139B

Mariana walks out of the bathroom dressed in her mother's
slip. She stands for a moment outside her parent's room and
seems to think something. Then she opens the door and walks
inside.

139C   INT. BEDROOM, GINA'S HOUSE -- NIGHT   139C

She finds Santiago sitting in the bed, scrutinizing the place.
When she comes in, Santiago points to the bed.

>   SANTIAGO
>   Lie down here.

Mariana obeys and lies on her mother's side. Santiago takes
off his boots and lies down on the other side. He turns off
the lamp. They remain silent in the room lit by the moon.
We can only hear their nervous inhalations.

>   SANTIAGO (CONT'D)
>   Does your burn hurt?

>   MARIANA
>   A little.

>   SANTIAGO
>   Mine hurts a lot.

They both smile. Santiago reaches out and strokes her hair.
She allows it. He lowers his hand and caresses her neck.

>   MARIANA
>   You said you wouldn't touch me.

He lowers his hand a little more and brushes against her
breasts. She does not protest. He moves over and puts his
face next to hers.

>   SANTIAGO
>   Do you want me to go?

She shakes her head. Santiago starts to kiss her.

140   EXT. SANTIAGO'S HOUSE, CIUDAD VICTORIA -- MORNING   140

Dawn. A Nissan pickup truck parks in the driveway of a humble
one-floor house in a lower-middle class neighborhood.

Carlos gets out of the truck. She looks very upset and doesn't
gets out.

He goes to the fence and sees she is still inside the car.
Goes back to her and opens the door.

>   CARLOS
>   María no tengo tiempo para estarme
>   peleando contigo ahorita si?
>   (MORE)

(CONTINUED)

140   CONTINUED: 140

>   CARLOS (CONT'D)
>   Por favor ya... [María, come on, I
>   got no time to argue with you ok?]

141   INT. SANTIAGO'S HOUSE, CIUDAD VICTORIA -- MORNING   141

They enter the house. Carlos turns around and gives her an
order.

>   CARLOS
>   Necesito que hagas una maleta con tu
>   ropa como para una semana. [I need
>   you to pack a suitcase with enough
>   clothes to last you a week.]

>   MARIA
>   Yo no voy a ningún lado. No pienso
>   conocer a sea señora.[I'm not going
>   anywhere. I don't want to meet her.]

>   CARLOS
>   María, solo métete a bañar y empaca
>   si? [Just pack your bag and take a
>   bath ok?]

>   MARIA
>   ¿Y si no quiero? [And if I don't
>   want to go?]

>   CARLOS
>   Es tu mamá.

>   MARIA
>   ¿Mi mamá? Nunca la he visto en toda

>   MARIA (CONT'D)
>   Mi vida. [My mom? I've never even
>   seen her.]

>   CARLOS
>   Pues vas a venir ¿ok? [You're coming
>   with me, ok?]

>   MARIA
>   ¡Chingados, que no! [Fuck, I don't
>   want to go!]

Carlos holds back and turns to confront her.

(CONTINUED)

141   CONTINUED: 141

                         CARLOS
             Ahora resulta, ¿Cuándo has oído a
             tu papá decir una sola grosería?
             [When did we teach you these bad
             words? When did you hear your father
             curse like that?]

     She leaves and locks herself inside her room.

                         CARLOS (CONT'D)
             Ahora empaca y metete a bañar que te
             vas a subir a ese avión quieras o no
             quieras. [You're getting on that
             plane with me. Now get a bath and
             pack your suitcase.]

     She shouts from inside the room.

                         MARIA
             No.

     Carlos tries to keep his cool.

142   INT. GINA'S CAR -- NIGHT   142

     Gina arrives home in her Pinto. Worried, she sees Robert's
     trailer parked outside her house.

143   INT. GINA'S HOUSE -- NIGHT   143

     Robert and the kids are watching television. Gina acts
     naturally while Mariana stares at her fixedly.

                         GINA
             Hey everybody, y'all had dinner yet?

     Robert and the kids don't answer, absorbed in the box. Mariana
     answers.

                         MARIANA
             No. We were waiting for you.

                         GINA
             I'll get right on it.

144   INT. KITCHEN, GINA'S HOUSE -- NIGHT   144

     Gina is focused on finding the ingredients in the pantry
     when Mariana walks in.

                         MARIANA
             Why are you so late?

                                                        (CONTINUED)

144   CONTINUED: 144

Mariana's sudden emergence startles Gina, who drops a can
and spills some flour.

                              GINA
                Honey, you scared me.

Gina starts to clean up the flour. Mariana leans on the
sink and stares to her mother.

                            MARIANA
                What did you do today?

                              GINA
                I stopped by to pick up the fabric
                and then went to Libby's.

                            MARIANA
                I went to Libby's too and I didn't
                see you there.

                              GINA
                Maybe you weren't there when I was.

                            MARIANA
                I was there since four o'clock.

They exchange glances. Mariana seems to be challenging her.

                              GINA
                All right now girl, stop askin'
                questions and help me clean up.

Mariana doesn't move. She just stares at her.

145   INT. ROOM, GINA'S HOUSE -- MORNING   145

Robert is asleep and snores. Gina is sitting on the edge of
her bed dressed in a slip, thinking. We hear voices in the
street. Gina looks out the window and sees her children
walking to school.

146   INT. HALLWAY, GINA'S HOUSE -- MORNING   146

Gina talks on the phone, nervously looking around.

                              GINA
                Nick, it's Gina. I need to talk to
                you... No, not at the trailer. I'll
                meet you at the supermarket at eleven.

She hangs up, then looks around again.

147   INT. SUPERMARKET -- DAY   147

Gina pushes a cart with some items in it. Nick peers into
one of the aisles. With her head, Gina signals the dairy
section at the end of the aisle.

148   INT. DAIRY SECTION, SUPERMARKET -- DAY   148

Nick approaches Gina.

                    NICK
          What happened?

                    GINA
          I think we're going too far.

                    NICK
          What're you talking about?

Gina remains silent when she sees two older women approach.
She feigns ignorance among the yogurt until they leave.

                    GINA
          I think my daughter knows.

                    NICK
          How could she know?

                    GINA
          Nick, a river can't run in two
          directions at once.

                    NICK
          Those are the lyrics to a really bad
          song. What we have is special.

                    GINA
          I want to stop seeing you. It's not
          right.

                    NICK
          I love you, you love me. I don't
          know if this is right, but is real.
          Are you gonna let it go?

                    GINA
          Nick, understand.

                    NICK
          Answer me, are you gonna let it go?

Gina nods. She looks sad, but decided.

                              (CONTINUED)

148   CONTINUED: 148

> **GINA**
> Yes, I won't see you anymore.

Nick looks at her straight in the eyes.

> **NICK**
> Forever?

> **GINA**
> Nick, I can't keep seeing you.

> **NICK**
> I'm gonna wait for you at the trailer
> every day at noon until you come
> back.

Nick steps forward and kisses her. She responds, keeping an
eye out while she kisses him. They separate, and he turns
and leaves.

149   INT. KITCHEN, GINA'S HOUSE -- DAY   149

Gina sits alone, waiting at the kitchen table. She hears
something and goes to see: Robert, Bobby and Monnie have
arrived. Gina gets up to greet them.

> **MONNIE**
> Hi mommy.

Gina hugs her and gives her a kiss. Bobby and Robert get
into the house.

> **GINA**
> I got y'all a surprise.

150   EXT. PATIO -- DAY   150

Gina opens the door. Laid out on a table in the patio are
sandwiches, potato chips and soda. Robert turns to Gina.

> **ROBERT**
> What's this?

> **GINA**
> It's been a while since we had a
> picnic.

> **ROBERT**
> In the patio? It's cold out here.

151   EXT. PATIO -- LATER   151

Robert and Gina eat their sandwiches, sitting on white plastic
chairs. Robert seems to be bored. The only ones having fun
are Bobby and Monnie, who are roasting marshmallows in the
grill .

Mariana and Pat enter into the patio. Gina stands up.

                    GINA
          Hi, come on in and join us.

Pat and Mariana look to each other.

                    PAT
          Why are we having a party?

                    GINA
          It's not a party. Just a picnic.
          For the fun of it.

The idea seems to horrify Pat.

                    PAT
          I have homework to do mom.

                    GINA
          Don't you want to roast marshmallows?

                    PAT
          I'm not a kid anymore, mom.

Pat turns to leave away, leaving Mariana by herself.

                    GINA
                 (To Mariana)
          What about you?

                    MARIANA
          I gotta go to Cherry's house to work
          on a school project.

                    GINA
          Stay just a bit. Come on.

                    MARIANA
          No, really. I can't. I'll be back
          later. Bye dad.

She kisses her father goodbye, takes her bike and leaves the
patio.

151A   EXT. GINA'S HOUSE -- DAY   151A

Mariana leaves on her bike.

152   EXT. TRAILER HOME -- DAY   152

Mariana arrives at the trailer home. She parks her bike under a mesquite and approaches cautiously.

She knocks on the door. Nobody answers and she enters.

153   INT. TRAILER HOME -- DAY   153

Mariana examines the place. It is now neat and clean.

154   INT. ROOM, TRAILER HOME -- DAY   154

She goes to the room and sits on the bed. She walks over to the pillows and smells them. First one, then the other. She lies back. She looks around.

She gets up, smooths out the covers and leaves.

155   INT. ROOM, GINA'S HOUSE -- NIGHT   155

Gina, in her slip, and Robert with a t shirt and his underwear down, are making love.

His rhythm is mechanical and monotonous. Robert strokes her chest, and when he does he touches her scar. He stops and dismounts.

> ROBERT
> I can't do this...

He strokes her hair, gently.

> ROBERT (CONT'D)
> I just can't...I'm sorry...

He kisses her softly on the forehead. Then turns aside and grabs her hand. Gina, without saying a word, just stares at him, frustrated.

156   OMITTED   156

157   INT. LAURA'S APARTMENT -- DAY   157

Laura is watching T.V. in the living room of her small apartment. Someone knocks loudly on the door.

(CONTINUED)

157   CONTINUED: 157

                          LAURA
                 Coming.

The knocking continues. Laura gets up, annoyed, and opens.
She finds Sylvia, completely devastated.

                          LAURA (CONT'D)
                 Are you ok?

Sylvia just stares at her and shakes her head.

158   EXT. HOTEL -- NIGHT   158

Laura's car is parked outside a hotel. Sylvia is leaning on
the hood, smoking nervously. It's drizzling lightly.

Laura exits the hotel and walks toward her.

                          LAURA
                 There's no one that fits their
                 description in this hotel either.
                 Let's check the Lincoln Inn.

Sylvia hangs her head, dejected.

                          SYLVIA
                 We're not going to find her. She's
                 gone.

                          LAURA
                 Look, we've only checked five hotels.
                 We're going to find her. Believe me,
                 a Mexican with a 12 year old girl is
                 not easy to hide. We just need to
                 keep on looking.

Sylvia gives her cigarette a long drag without looking at
Laura.

                          LAURA (CONT'D)
                 How long since you've seen your
                 daughter?

                          SYLVIA
                 I left her two days after she was
                 born.

Laura turns to look at her, disconcerted.

                          LAURA
                 Why?

                                              (CONTINUED)

158   CONTINUED: 158

Sylvia turns and stares at her before answering.

                    SYLVIA
            Because I didn't deserve her.

159   EXT. SANTIAGO'S HOUSE -- DAY   159

Santiago parks his truck in the garage and gets out. He is
carrying some supermarket bags.

159A   OMITTED   159A

160   INT. SANTIAGO'S HOUSE -- DAY   160

Santiago enters the house and sees Mariana drinking coffee
with Ana and Paula. Santiago stops dead in his tracks when
he sees her.

                    ANA
            Hi hon. There's somebody here to see
            you.

Santiago and Mariana's eyes meet.

                    MARIANA
            Hi.

                    PAULA
            You never told us about Mariana.

                    SANTIAGO
            She's a friend from school.

He puts the supermarket bags in the kitchen and walks toward
them.

                    ANA
            Are you gonna stay for lunch, darlin'?

                    MARIANA
            No, thanks.

                    SANTIAGO
            Were gonna grab lunch somewhere else.

                    ANA
                (To Santiago)
            Ok, so I'm goin' to Paula's house
            for lunch.
                (To Mariana)
            Good to meet you.

                                                      (CONTINUED)

160   CONTINUED: 160

Paula looks discreetly to Santiago and with her eyes points
to Mariana, smiling.

                        PAULA
            See you later. Have fun.

Ana and Paula leave. Santiago stands in front of Mariana.

                        SANTIAGO
            What're you doing here?

                        MARIANA
            I want to see your parent's room.

161   INT. ROOM, NICK'S HOUSE -- DAY   161

They enter. Mariana looks around the room. She observes some
family photos: Santiago when he was three years old, Cristobal
and Santiago as kids, Nick and Ana together.

                        MARIANA
            Did your mom and dad get along?

                        SANTIAGO
            So so.

Mariana sits on the bed.

                        MARIANA
            Come here.

Santiago locks the door and sits beside her. Mariana points
at the burn on his arm.

                        MARIANA (CONT'D)
            Still hurt?

                        SANTIAGO
            Nah.

Without another word, Mariana gets up and undresses. Santiago
hugs her and kisses her belly. Mariana holds him away.

                        MARIANA
            Would you marry me?

In answer, Santiago throws her onto the bed and starts to
kiss her all over.

162   EXT. RUNWAY AIRPORT CITY OREGON -- DAY   162

The plane touches down on the airport runway.

163   EXT. CAR RENTAL AGENCY -- EVENING   163

Carlos drives an Ikon out in the middle of a downpour.

164   INT. HOTEL ROOM -- EVENING   164

Carlos and Maria enter a cheap motel room with two single
beds. Carlos puts the suitcases to one side.

                    CARLOS
          ¿Te gusta? [How do you like it?]

                    MARIA
          Hace frío. [It's cold.]

Carlos studies the heater and cranks it up.

                    CARLOS
          Listo, ahorita se calienta el cuarto.
          [Done. The room'll warm up in a bit.]

Maria just sits on one of the beds. Then grabs the remote
and turns on the T.V. She flicks through the channels while
Carlos unpacks his clothes into the closet.

                    MARIA
          ¿Tú conociste a mi mamá? [Did you
          meet my mother?]

                    CARLOS
          No, cuando conocí a tu papá tu mamá
          ya los había dejado. [No. I met your
          dad after she'd left.]

                    MARIA
          ¿Por qué nos dejó? [Why did she leave
          us?]

                    CARLOS
          No sé. Tu papá trató de encontrarla
          varias veces. Supo donde estaba hasta
          hace poco. [I don't know. Your dad
          tried to find her several times. He
          didn't find her until recently.]

                    MARIA
          No quiero conocerla. Ya hay que
          regresarnos. [I don't want to meet
          here. Let's go back.]

164   CONTINUED: 164

                        CARLOS
            No podemos, le juré a tu papá que la
            encontraríamos. Y la vamos a
            encontrar. [We can't. I swore to
            your dad that we'd find her. And
            we're going to find her.]

165   INT. HOTEL ROOM -- NIGHT   165

They lie in bed with the light off. Maria's eyes are open.

                        MARIA
            ¿Estás despierto? [You awake?]

                        CARLOS
            Mmhh.

                        MARIA
            Si se muere mi papá ¿me vas a dejar
            aquí con mi mamá? [If my dad dies,
            are you going to leave me here with
            my mom?]

Maria's eyes brim with tears.

                        CARLOS
            Ya te dije que tu papá no se va a
            morir. [I already told you, your
            dad's not going to die.]

                        MARIA
            No me vayas a dejar con mi mamá, por
            favor. [Don't leave me with me my
            mom, please.]

165A   OMITTED   165A

166   EXT. SYLVIA'S APARTMENT -- DAY   166

Carlos is leaning against a wall, waiting. He is watching
people passing by, cars crossing the street.

Suddenly Sylvia walks out into the street. She is wearing a
simple blue cotton dress with her hair let down. Carlos pays
attention to her. She walks down the street toward the corner.
Carlos follows her with his eyes, from a distance. A Honda
Civic pulls up beside her and she gets in.

167   INT. GINA'S HOUSE -- DAY   167

Gina is alone in the living room vacuuming. She looks at the
clock: 11:56 a.m. She thinks for a moment and then she
continues her task.

168   EXT. GARDEN, GINA'S HOUSE -- DAY   168

She is sitting on a bench in the garden drinking a cup of
tea, pensive.

She raises her face to the bright sun and closes her eyes.

168A   OMITTED   168A

169   INT. ROOM, GINA'S HOUSE -- NIGHT   169

Robert is asleep. Gina, awake, cries quietly.

169A   OMITTED   169A

170   INT. LAUNDRY ROOM, GINA'S HOUSE -- DAY   170

Gina is ironing some of Robert's shirts, absorbed in her
chores. She looks into the living room at the clock: 11:58
a.m. Gina unplugs the iron and leaves.

171   EXT. ENVIRONS TRAILER HOME -- DAY   171

Gina's Pinto tears down the path.

172   INT. GINA'S CAR -- DAY   172

Through the windshield, in the distance, Gina sees Nick's
truck leaving.

Gina accelerates and honks repeatedly. Nick's truck stops.

172A   OMITTED   172A

173   EXT. TRUCK -- DAY   173

Gina parks the Pinto beside his truck. Nick walks toward
her, and she immediately gets out of the car.

                         GINA
               Don't ever leave me again. Never,
               never, never...

He walks toward her and hugs her.

174   EXT. TRAILER HOME -- DAY   174

The truck and the Pinto are parked before the trailer home.
Mariana emerges amid the mesquites and approaches carefully.
She reaches the home. Backed up against the trailer walls,
she sidles up the window of the room her mother is in.

She looks around and sees a 19 gallon plastic bucket. She
carries it to the window and looks in. Through the blinds
she sees her mother and Nick making love and her face grows
pale. She climbs down and silently walks away.

175   INT. TRAILER HOME -- DAY   175

Gina sits on the bed, thinking, while Nick finishes dressing.

                    GINA
          D' you have to go back to the factory.

                    NICK
          Yeah, I've got the night shift again.
          I'm sick of it, I wish I could change
          my life, go live somewhere else.

Nick's answer sets Gina thinking.

                    GINA
          Would you take me with you?

Nick doesn't hesitate to answer.

                    NICK
          Yes.

Gina is surprised.

                    GINA
          You'd leave your family for me?

                    NICK
          I wouldn't think about it. My kids
          are grownups now... You?

Gina mulls over her answer, staring at the worn carpet.

                    GINA
          My kids are younger.

                    NICK
          Would you?

Gina looks back at the carpet and slowly nods.

175A   OMITTED   175A

176   EXT. LINCOLN INN -- NIGHT   176

Laura's car is parked in the parking lot of a cheap motel.
At the entrance a sign reads 29.99 a night - Free Cable
T.V.

Sylvia is leaning on the hood. Laura runs up to her.

                    LAURA
          They're in room 14.

177   EXT. ROOM 14, LINCOLN INN -- NIGHT   177

Room 14 is on the second floor, far from the stairs. The
Ikon is parked below, in the parking lot. Laura and Sylvia
wait outside the door. Sylvia looks anxious.

Laura knocks on the door. No one opens. She knocks again.
Carlos opens barefoot, dressed in jeans and a t-shirt, and
stares at them inquisitively.

                    CARLOS
          ¿Y ahora tú qué quieres?   [What d'you
          want?]

Sylvia looks at Carlos and then exchanges a glance with Laura.

                    SYLVIA
          I want to see my daughter.

                    CARLOS
          No te entiendo. [I can't understand
          you.]

Laura intervenes with terrible Spanish.

                    LAURA
          Ella quiere ver hija. [She wants see
          daughter.]

From inside the room, Maria shouts.

                    MARIA
          No la quiero ver. [I don't want to
          see her.]

Carlos turns toward Sylvia.

                                        (CONTINUED)

177   CONTINUED: 177

                         CARLOS
              No te quiere ver. [She doesn't want
              to see you.]

                         MARIA
              Dile que se vaya. [Tell her to go
              away.]

                         CARLOS
              La dejaste parada en la pinche calle
              y ahora te chingas. [You left her
              standing in the street so fuck off.]

Carlos closes the door. Sylvia and Laura stand there without
knowing what to do. The rain intensifies. Sylvia looks at
the dark sky.

Sylvia sees her doubtful. Laura tries to calm her down.

                         LAURA
              Don't worry, we will figure something
              out.

177A   EXT. HOTEL HALL -- DAY   177A

Sylvia and Laura get into a room that faces opposite the
room where Carlos and Maria are.

177B   INT. ROOM, MOTEL LINCOLN INN -- DAY   177B

Sylvia pulls out a chair and sits before the open door
checking the room of Maria and Carlos, just opposite in the
other side of the hallway.

177C   INT. ROOM, MOTEL LINCOLN INN -- NIGHT   177C

Sylvia is still sitting in the chair. Laura is in bed, under
the covers, asleep.

Sylvia stares through the open door, watching the room across
the hall.

177D   INT. ROOM MOTEL LINCOLN INN -- DAY   177D

Sylvia sits in the chair, completely asleep. The door is
still open.

She listens to some noise: the doors of a car opening. She
wakes up and glances at the door. In the parking lot is Carlos
putting his luggage in the trunk of his rental car.

177E   EXT. ROOM MOTEL LINCOLN INN -- DAY   177E

Sylvia goes out of the room and checks the car. Maria doesn't seems to be with him. Sylvia notices that the door of Maria's room is open. She walks toward the room.

While she is getting in Carlos notices her and shouts at her.

>   CARLOS
>   ¿Adónde vas? [Where you going?]

She gets in. Carlos climbs the stairs quickly.

177F   INT. MARIA'S ROOM MOTEL -- DAY   177F

Maria is packing her clothes when she sees Sylvia coming in. She looks surprised.

>   SYLVIA
>   Please, give me two minutes.

Maria doesn't answer.

>   SYLVIA (CONT'D)
>   Let me explain to you.

Carlos comes into the room with his key and stares at Sylvia.

>   CARLOS
>   ¿Qué chingados quieres? [What the
>   fuck do you want?]

Sylvia keeps talking to Maria. Laura glances through the open door.

>   SYLVIA
>   Maria, I need to talk to you.

Carlos confronts her.

>   CARLOS
>   Déjala en paz. [Leave her alone.]

Sylvia looks Maria directly in her eyes.

>   SYLVIA
>   I'm sorry. Really sorry. Let me talk
>   to you for two minutes, only two
>   minutes.

Maria and Carlos exchange a glance.

(CONTINUED)

177F   CONTINUED: 177F

>   CARLOS
>   Quieres hablar con ella? [Do you
>   want to talk to her?]

>   MARIA
>   Carlos, Carlos...

He doesn't pay attention to her. He continues confronting
Sylvia.

>   CARLOS
>   Ahora si quieres hablar con ella.

>   MARIA
>   Carlos.

He turns to Maria, angry.

>   CARLOS
>   Qué? [What?]

>   MARIA
>   Déjala. [Leave her alone.]

>   CARLOS
>   Estás segura mi hija? [Are you sure
>   sweetheart?]

Maria nods. Carlos goes out of the room, leaving them alone.
Maria sits on one of the beds. Sylvia closes the door.

>   SYLVIA
>   I'm really sorry for running away
>   like that yesterday, it's just...

Maria looks up, observes her briefly, then looks back down.
She remains silent. Sylvia points at the other bed.

>   SYLVIA (CONT'D)
>   Do you mind if I sit down?

Maria just looks at her and doesn't answer. Sylvia goes to
sit on the bed across from her. She looks nervous.

>   SYLVIA (CONT'D)
>   Do you speak English?

Maria looks up, stares at her and nods.

>   SYLVIA (CONT'D)
>   You're all grown up.
>   (MORE)

(CONTINUED)

177F CONTINUED: (2)   177F

> SYLVIA (CONT'D)
> I always used to think of you on
> your birthdays, and I'd try to imagine
> what you looked like.

Maria doesn't say a word. Sylvia's nervousness grows.

> SYLVIA (CONT'D)
> You're very beautiful, you know?

Maria looks at her with no emotion.

> SYLVIA (CONT'D)
> You look like your father.

Listening to this, Maria's expression changes.

> MARIA
> My dad's in the hospital.

Sylvia looks amazed to hear her daughter speaking, at the
same time she learns that Santiago is ill.

> SYLVIA
> What happened to him?

> MARIA
> He crashed his plane.

> SYLVIA
> How is he?

Maria shrugs. Sylvia tries to reach her hand toward Maria,
but she leans back avoiding her.

Sylvia looks confused, she doesn't know how to react.

> SYLVIA (CONT'D)
> He's a pilot?

The question seems to bother Maria. She answers dryly.

> MARIA
> He's a crop duster. You didn't know?

Sylvia shakes her head. Another uncomfortable silence.

177G OMITTED   177G

178   EXT. LINCOLN INN -- NIGHT   178

Carlos is leaning against the guardrail in the hallway.
Laura is standing next to him. The door opens and Sylvia
walks out. Then Maria.

> CARLOS
> (To Maria)
> Todo bien? [Everything ok?]

Maria nods.

> CARLOS (CONT'D)
> Tu papá me pidió que la trajera de
> vuelta a México con nosotros. ¿Tú
> quieres que venga? [Your dad asked
> me to bring her back to Mexico with
> us. Do you want her to come?]

Maria remains pensive for a moment and nods, though not
entirely convinced.

179   EXT. SANTIAGO'S HOUSE -- DAY   179

Santiago is washing the truck, with the radio on, listening
to a country song. Suddenly, a hand turns off the radio.
Santiago, who's been soaping up one of the tires, looks up
to see what happened.

Xavier and Cristobal are standing over him, staring. Cristobal
seems calm.

> CRISTOBAL
> The girl you brought home the other
> day, is her daughter?

Santiago stands up holding the soapy brush.

> SANTIAGO
> Yes.

> CRISTOBAL
> Are you fucking her?

Santiago doesn't answer. Cristobal looks around.

> CRISTOBAL (CONT'D)
> Why you do it?

> SANTIAGO
> It's none of your business.

(CONTINUED)

                              XAVIER
               You can't do this shit to your mom.

With a gesture of his hand, Cristobal silences him.

                            CRISTOBAL
               You stay out of this. It isn't enough
               what already happened?

Santiago doesn't answer.

                         CRISTOBAL (CONT'D)
               Tell me.

                            SANTIAGO
               This has nothing to do with you.

Cristobal smiles sardonically.

                            CRISTOBAL
               You're gonna stop seeing her. You
               understand?
                    (A beat)
               Do you understand?

Cristobal and Xavier walk away. Santiago stares at them.

180   EXT. TRUCK -- LATER   180

Santiago and Mariana are lying, staring at the sky.

                            MARIANA
               You know, when I was little I used
               to think the sun could melt me.

                            SANTIAGO
               Like an ice cream cone?

                            MARIANA
               Uh huh. I thought that sweat was my
               flesh turning into water.

They both smile.

                         MARIANA (CONT'D)
               What d'you think your dad and my mom
               talked about?

                            SANTIAGO
               I dunno, the weather, music...

180   CONTINUED: 180

                         MARIANA
               D'you think they talked about us?

                         SANTIAGO
               Maybe... I don't know.

They remain silent for a moment. Mariana turns and kisses
him tenderly on the cheek. He looks at her, surprised.

                         MARIANA
               D'you think they didn't use a condom,
               like us?

                         SANTIAGO
               Yeah.

                         MARIANA
               They say that if you make love with
               real passion, the sperm burns and
               die before they reach the egg.

                         SANTIAGO
               Like they were melted by the sun?

Maria smiles and remains pensive. Then she turns to kiss
him.

181   EXT. SANTIAGO'S HOUSE -- EVENING   181

Santiago's pickup truck parks in the garage. Santiago gets
out and walks toward his house. Suddenly, from the darkened
porch, we hear a voice.

                         ANA (O.S.)
               Do you enjoy betraying your family?

Santiago squints in the dark. He can barely make out his
mother's face.

                         ANA (O.S.) (CONT'D)
               I'm talking to you, you son of a
               bitch.

Santiago turns on a light and sees his drunken mother sunk
into one of the worn porch sofas.

                         SANTIAGO
               I didn't betray anyone.

                                                       (CONTINUED)

181   CONTINUED: 181

                              ANA
                   You're worse than your father: you
                   even dared to bring her home. You're
                   going to be buried in hell with him.

        Santiago stares at her, deeply moved.

                              SANTIAGO
                   I'm sorry.

        Santiago turns and walks indoors.

182   INT. LIVING ROOM, GINA'S HOUSE -- NIGHT   182

        Pat and Monnie are watching t.v. Suddenly we hear the loud
        crash of shattering glass, and a large rock wrapped in paper
        lands next to Monnie, who screams, frightened.

                              MONNIE
                   Ahh!

        Pat runs to look out the broken window and sees a truck
        speeding away.

        Pat picks up the rock and opens the piece of paper. He reads
        "Santiago Martinez is fucking your daughter Mariana."

        Robert walks into the living room.

                              ROBERT
                   What happened?

        Pat shows him the piece of paper.

183   INT. MARIANA'S ROOM -- NIGHT   183

        Robert stands before Mariana, humiliated and indignant. She
        only listens.

                              ROBERT
                   Tell me it ain't true.

        Mariana says nothing, stays silent. Robert holds the piece
        of paper up to her face.

                              ROBERT (CONT'D)
                   Tell me this is a lie.

        Mariana looks at the piece of paper and doesn't answer.

                              ROBERT (CONT'D)
                   Did you actually sleep with him?

                                                       (CONTINUED)

Mariana just looks at him. Robert takes this as a yes, and
immediately starts rabidly slapping Mariana. She resists
with a certain dignity.

                    ROBERT (CONT'D)
              You're a whore. How dare you?

Robert seems incapable of stopping. Each blow is fiercer
than the last. Mariana resists fearlessly.

                    ROBERT (CONT'D)
              I'm gonna kill him.

Robert storms out. After a while, Mariana also leaves.

184   INT. LIVING ROOM, GINA'S HOUSE -- NIGHT   184

All her siblings have been listening, frightened, from the
living room. The father rushes out and slams the door.
Mariana crosses the living room, opens the door and watches
her father get into the van and leave.

She spins around, walks past her brothers and heads for her
father's bedroom.

185   INT. ROOM, GINA'S HOUSE -- NIGHT   185

Mariana enters the room and locks it. She goes straight to
the phone and dials.

                    SANTIAGO (O.S.)
              Hello.

                    MARIANA
              Santiago. My dad is on his way to
              kill you.

There is an urgency in her voice.

                    SANTIAGO (O.S.)
              What are you talking about?

                    MARIANA
              He left in the van to go find you.
              Get out of there and come get me,
              let's leave together.

                    SANTIAGO (O.S.)
              Ok. I'm coming right now.

185A EXT. MAROMA'S STREETS -- NIGHT   185A

Robert's van crosses at full speed some of the streets.

185B OMITTED   185B

186   EXT. AIRPORT, CIUDAD VICTORIA -- DAY   186

The plane lands at Ciudad Victoria airport.

186A OMITTED   186A

187   INT. TRUCK -- DAY   187

The three ride in the Nissan truck. Sylvia, in front, smokes
nervously with the window open. Anxious, she gazes at the
Tamaulipan landscape.

188   EXT. HOSPITAL -- DAY   188

They park outside the hospital. They get out and Carlos heads
toward the entrance. Sylvia looks at the place and takes
Maria by the arm as she is about to go in.

                         SYLVIA
              I'll catch up with you in a second.

Maria locks eyes with Sylvia.

                         MARIA
                   Ok.

Maria walks away. Sylvia leans against the car. She rubs her
head with both hands and takes a deep breath.

188A OMITTED   188A

189   EXT. ENVIRONS, TRAILER HOME -- DAY   189

At a distance, Mariana watches how her mother and Nick give
each other a long kiss goodbye, then get in their cars.

Mariana quickly hides when she sees her mother's Pinto coming
toward her. It passes just some twenty yards away from her.

Mariana waits until both cars drive away and as soon as they
do, she heads over to the trailer home.

190   EXT. TRAILER HOME -- MOMENTS LATER   190

Mariana opens the door and looks around to make sure nobody
is watching her. She enters.

190A   INT. TRAILER HOME -- DAY   190A

Mariana explores the trailer. She stops to look around. She examines the sofas, the kitchen. Then she walks towards the bedroom.

191   INT. ROOM, TRAILER HOME -- DAY   191

She stops in front of the bed. It is still wrinkled with its pillows ruffled after Nick and Gina made love. She looks at the bed with curiosity and anger.

191A   EXT. TRAILER HOME -- DAY   191A

Mariana goes out of the trailer. She looks disturbed, hurt. She circles the home, inspecting the exterior. She stops in front of the gas tank. She follows the connections and finds one close to the bathroom.

She fiddles with the copper pipe until she breaks it. Immediately the gas begins to escape out.

Hurriedly she goes to the tank and closes the valve. The gas stops leaking out. She opens it again and again the gas escapes into the desert air.

She closes the valve and sits beside the tank, her gaze lost in the vast plain.

191B   OMITTED   191B

192   INT. MARIANA'S ROOM -- NIGHT   192

Gina is sitting on Monnie's bed. Monnie is praying.

                    MONNIE
          And that you take care of us and
          everybody else... Amen...

Gina blesses her and then goes to Mariana's bed.

                    GINA
          You prayed yet?

                  MARIANA
          No, I don't pray anymore.

                    GINA
          That's wrong, Mariana.

(CONTINUED)

                    MARIANA
          There are lots of things that are
          wrong, mom, and that can't be fixed
          by praying.

                    GINA
          You've been actin' real strange.
          Tomorrow, I want to hear what's on
          your mind.

Gina blesses her and walks out.

                    MONNIE
          Is it true you don't pray anymore?

                    MARIANA
          Yes.

                    MONNIE
          Why?

                    MARIANA
          Because God never listens.

193   EXT. GINA'S HOUSE -- NIGHT   193

       All the lights are off. Total silence. We hear a door slowly
       open. Mariana walks out with a bag in her hand and goes toward
       the patio storage room.

194   INT. GARAGE -- NIGHT   194

       Mariana walks in, closes the door and turns on the light.
       From behind some boxes she pulls out of a can of gasoline,
       and from her bag she takes out a ball of yarn. She cuts five
       yards of yarn and soaks it in gasoline.

       She walks out of the storage room towards the patio.

194A   EXT. PATIO, GINA'S HOUSE -- NIGHT   194A

       She goes to the grill. Turns on the propane gas tank and
       lets some gas escape from the burners for a while. She turns
       it off and then she walks a few steps laying out the yarn.
       She lights it, the yarn catches fire and when the fire reaches
       the end a great flame emerges into the air.

       Mariana seems to be satisfied with her experiment.

195   INT. HOSPITAL -- AFTERNOON   195

Sylvia and Maria wait together. Carlos sits a few seats away.
Three peasants - their faces wrinkled from endless hours
working in the sun - sit before them. The eldest naps with
his mouth open. Sylvia watches him uneasily.

                    SYLVIA
          What grade are you in?

Maria answers without looking at her.

                    MARIA
          I'm in eighth grade.

The dryness of Maria's answers seems to discourage Sylvia,
but she is determined to establish a conversation with her.

                    SYLVIA
          Do you have a boyfriend?

                    MARIA
          No.
               (A beat)
          Do you have one?

                    SYLVIA
          No, I dont.

An uncomfortable silence. Maria stares at one of the walls.
A nurse enters and calls out loud.

                    NURSE
          José Sánchez Martínez.

The peasants get up. They wake up the older and help him
stand. Sylvia hadn't noticed that he has a long gash on his
arm that is still bleeding.

Impressed, she follows them with her eyes until they enter
the emergency room. Sylvia turns to Maria.

                    SYLVIA
          Come, let's go get something to eat.

                    MARIA
          No, I want to stay here with my dad.

                    SYLVIA
          You haven't eaten anything all day.

Maria looks at her. Sylvia stands up.

                                        (CONTINUED)

195   CONTINUED: 195

                         SYLVIA (CONT'D)
          We'll be back soon.

196   EXT. PLAZA -- AFTERNOON   196

Maria and Sylvia walk around a plaza near the hospital.

Sylvia looks around. Life bustles about the hospital: street
vendors, pedestrians, balloon salesmen, transit cops
exaggeratedly waving at cars, stray dogs waiting for scraps.

                           SYLVIA
          Did you like growing up here?

                           MARIA
          Yeah. There are good people here.

                           SYLVIA
          And Carlos, who is he?

                           MARIA
          He's my dad's best friend.

Sylvia notices a churro cart. She stops.

                           SYLVIA
          Churros. Do you want one?

                           MARIA
          No thanks.

Sylvia seems not to pay attention to Maria's answer. She
turns to the vendor and asks for the churros in bad Spanish.

                        MARIA (CONT'D)
          Dos por favor. [Give me two, please.]

The vendor gives them the churros and Sylvia pays.

                           SYLVIA
          I haven't had churros for many, many
          years. I used to love them. When I
          was your age, my dad drove us every
          Thanksgiving to Juarez just to have
          churros.

Sylvia bites her churro and closes her eyes.

                         SYLVIA (CONT'D)
          This is like going back in time.

                                             (CONTINUED)

196 CONTINUED: 196

She opens her eyes and looks around: there's life everywhere.
Maria just stares at her in silence.

                    SYLVIA (CONT'D)
          I remember that Monnie always wanted
          a balloon and my mom...

                    MARIA
          Who is Monnie?

Maria's question stops Sylvia in her tracks. Suddenly she
realizes that the girl who is beside her is basically a
complete stranger to her.

                    SYLVIA
          Monnie is my younger sister.

They are silent a moment.

                    MARIA
          Do I have any aunts, uncles or cousins
          on your side?

Sylvia thinks about her answer before going on.

                    SYLVIA
          I don't know. I really don't know.

197 EXT. TRAILER HOME -- DAY   197

Gina waits for Nick sitting on the steps to the trailer home.
Nick's pickup approaches. While Nick parks, Gina stands up
to greet him.

197A OMITTED   197A

198 INT. ROOM, TRAILER HOME -- DAY   198

Nick and Gina are hugging on the bed, naked.

                    GINA
          D'you think I'm pretty?

                    NICK
          I think you're real pretty.

                    GINA
          I am going to have plastic surgery
          done on my breast.

                    NICK
          Don't do it, I like how you look.

                                        (CONTINUED)

198   CONTINUED: 198

                              GINA
                    But the scar looks awful.

He raises his head to look her at her eyes.

                              NICK
                    You beat death. You fought and won.
                    That makes your scar beautiful.
                    Don't erase it.

As an answer, she hugs him and starts kissing him.

199   OMITTED   199

199A   EXT. TRAILER HOME -- DAY   199A

While Nick and Gina make love, gas starts leaking through
the pipes. A fuse lights up and runs toward the pipes. The
bushes and grass beneath the trailer catch fire.

200   EXT. TRAILER HOME -- DAY   200

Mariana watches the flames, which are slowly burning the
trailer. She seems to wait for them coming out. Suddenly,
the flame travels through the pipe toward the gas tanks.
Mariana gets scared: this is not what she was planning.

                              MARIANA
                         (mumbling)
                    Mom...get out...

The tanks catch fire. She gives a step forward.

                         MARIANA   (mumbling)
                    Get out mom...get out mom...

Unexpectedly we hear a tremendous explosion, followed almost
immediately by another. The explosion knocks down Mariana.
The home burns quickly; the flames rise skyward. Mariana
stares at the burning trailer, completely shocked.

200A   OMITTED   200A

201   EXT. ENVIRONS, TRAILER HOME -- DAY   201

We see the trailer home burning in the distance. From far
away.

202   INT. HOSPITAL -- EVENING   202

It is getting dark. Sylvia leans on a doorframe, smoking as
she watches some moths flutter around a streetlamp.

                                                    (CONTINUED)

202   CONTINUED: 202

A doctor arrives and Carlos and Maria get up immediately.
Sylvia notices, takes a last, hurried drag and walks over.

                    CARLOS
            ¿Cómo sigue? [How is he doing?]

Before answering, the doctor glances at Maria.

                    DOCTOR
            ¿La niña puede escuchar? [It's ok if
            she hears?]

Carlos nods.

                    CARLOS
            Es su papá. [He's her father.]

The doctor continues.

                    DOCTOR
            El cuadro del paciente se complicó.
            Vamos a tener que operarlo. Si la
            infección es más grave de lo que
            pensamos, quizá sea necesario
            amputarle la pierna. [The patient
            has had some complications. We're
            going to have to operate. If the
            infection is worse than we thought,
            we may have to amputate his leg.]

Carlos is struck by the news. Maria cries quietly. Sylvia,
without understanding the conversation, doesn't know what to
do.

                    CARLOS
            ¿Podemos verlo? [Can we see him?]

                    DOCTOR
            Sí, pueden pasar a verlo unos minutos.
            Pero está dormido, sedado. [Yes,
            you can go see him for a few minutes,
            but he's asleep, sedated.]

203   INT. HOSPITAL ROOM -- NIGHT   203

The three enter the room followed by the doctor. Santiago
sleeps hooked up to several machines. His destroyed leg
lies outside the sheets. We can see the wounds, the sutures,
the spillage.

Sylvia contemplates Santiago, stunned. She looks at him from
top to bottom, as if she wants to recognize him.

                                              (CONTINUED)

Maria walks up to her father and tries to kiss him.

The doctor gets upset at her.

>   DOCTOR
>   No hija, no te acerques. [Don't get
>   close to him honey.]

Maria refrains herself. Then she turns to her mother.

>   MARIA
>   He's going to be ok, right?

Sylvia is surprised that her daughter should be asking her.

>   SYLVIA
>   Yeah, he's going to be ok.

Maria kisses her father again.

>   MARIA
>   I love you daddy.

She steps back and looks at him. The doctor ushers them out.

>   DOCTOR
>   No pueden estar aquí, tienen que
>   salir. [You can`t stay here, you
>   have to leave.]

Carlos takes her hand.

>   CARLOS
>   Vámonos mija, luego regresamos. [Come
>   on, we will return later.]

The girl looks at her father for another moment and turns to
leave. Sylvia remains motionless. She turns to the doctor
and tries to speak in very bad Spanish.

>   SYLVIA
>   Can I just stay for a little longer?

The doctor turns to Carlos.

>   DOCTOR
>   No le entiendo ¿Qué dijo? [What did
>   she say? I can't understand her]

Carlos looks at Sylvia for a moment.

>   CARLOS
>   Es su mujer, creo que se quiere quedar
>   un rato. [She's his wife. I think
>   she wants to stay for a little
>   longer.]

The doctor nods at Sylvia.

>   DOCTOR
>   Ok, dos minutos. [Ok, two minutes.]

The doctor, Carlos and Maria walk out. Sylvia closes the
door and approaches Santiago. Sylvia is disturbed to see
him: a whirlwind of memories seems to overwhelm her.

>   SYLVIA
>   Santiago, it's me... Mariana.

Santiago keeps breathing steadily. Sylvia grabs a chair from
the room and sits.

>   SYLVIA (CONT'D)
>   You are not going to die, are you?

Sylvia doesn't cry, but has trouble going on.

>   SYLVIA (CONT'D)
>   Because if you die I wouldn`t know
>   what do do with her.

She pauses, this hurts her.

>   SYLVIA (CONT'D)
>   I can barely look her in the eyes.

She looks at him, helpless.

>   SYLVIA (CONT'D)
>   She needs you, I need you.

She starts sobbing quietly.

>   SYLVIA (CONT'D)
>   I'm so scared. I've been scared of
>   myself and now I can't run away
>   anymore. I killed them. I killed
>   your father and my mother. I didn't
>   mean to but...now I can't get this
>   smell of them burning. I can't get
>   rid of it.

She stares at him, almost with anger.

                                                    (CONTINUED)

203   CONTINUED: (3)   203

> SYLVIA (CONT'D)
> Why did you make me come back here?
> Why?... Why?

204   INT. SANTIAGO'S HOUSE -- NIGHT   204

Santiago hangs up the phone and remains pensive for a moment.
He gets up and leaves the room.

205   INT. KITCHEN, SANTIAGO'S HOUSE -- NIGHT   205

He walks into the kitchen and finds Cristobal and Xavier
sitting at the kitchen table, smoking and drinking beer.

Ignoring them, Santiago looks for some keys on a rack. After
checking several, he doesn't find what he's looking for.

> SANTIAGO
> Where are the keys to the truck?

Cristobal turns to look at him sardonically.

> CRISTOBAL
> What d'you want them for?

> SANTIAGO
> What the fuck d'you care?

> CRISTOBAL
> Mom says you won't be driving it
> anymore, so why don't you ask her.

206   INT. ROOM, NICK'S HOUSE -- NIGHT   206

He opens the door and sees his mother lying down, with the
light from the nightstand on, watching t.v. He turns it off.

> SANTIAGO
> I need the keys to the truck.

Ana straightens up and sits on the edge of the bed.

> ANA
> You're not driving that truck anymore.
> In fact, you won't be living in this
> house anymore either.

Santiago doesn't budge.

> SANTIAGO
> Where are the keys.

206   CONTINUED: 206

                          ANA
              What d'you want them for? To go see
              your little whore?

Santiago pushes the television onto the floor, it breaks,
but the sound and image continue. Ana is frightened.

                       SANTIAGO
              Where are the keys?

Upon hearing the noise, Cristobal and Xavier enter the room.

                       CRISTOBAL
              What the fuck are you doing?

                       SANTIAGO
                  (screaming at Ana)
              Give me the keys, goddammit!

Ana opens a bedside drawer and throws them at him.

                          ANA
              Get out and don't ever come back.

Santiago catches them and is about to leave when Cristobal
gets in his way.

                       CRISTOBAL
              Where the fuck d'you think you're
              going?

Santiago pushes him so hard it knocks him over. Without
stopping, he steps around him and leaves the bedroom.

206A   INT. VAN -- NIGHT   206A

Robert is driving furiously. Slowly he begins to break down
until he stops.

206B   EXT. VAN -- NIGHT   206B

Robert's van parks beside the curb.

206C   INT. VAN -- NIGHT   206C

Robert looks around and suddenly he begins to cry, completely
crushed.

207   INT. TRUCK -- NIGHT   207

Santiago is driving full speed down the highway.

207A   EXT. MAROMA'S STREETS -- DAY   207A

Santiago drives his truck into the streets of Maroma.

207B   INT. TRUCK -- NIGHT   207B

Through the windshield Santiago observes Robert's van parked
a block from him. Santiago lowers his speed.

He turns to look at the van. Robert is there crying. They
exchange a glance: Robert is a defeated man.

Santiago slowly drives beside him without taking his eyes
from his and then he speeds off.

207C   INT. VAN -- NIGHT   207C

Robert sees how Santiago's truck heads toward his house.

207D   OMITTED   207D

208   INT. CAFETERIA -- NIGHT   208

Carlos, Maria and Sylvia are dining in silence at a local
cafeteria. For a long time no one talks, each one lost in
their thoughts. Maria's eyes are swollen from crying, and
rather than eat, she pushes a piece of bread around her plate.

>   MARIA
>   ¿Vamos a volver al hospital? [Are we
>   going back to the hospital?]

>   CARLOS
>   No, vamos a regresar a la casa. [No,
>   we're going back home.]

>   MARIA
>   Yo me quiero quedar con él. [I want
>   to stay with him.]

>   CARLOS
>   No, no tiene caso. Regresamos mañana
>   muy temprano. Necesitas descansar.
>   [No, there's no point. We'll come
>   back early in the morning.]

Carlos's answer weighs on her. She looks scared, confused,
hurt. Maria turns toward her mother.

>   MARIA
>   Are you going to stay with us?

(CONTINUED)

208   CONTINUED: 208

Sylvia looks at her.

209   INT. LIVING ROOM, SANTIAGO'S HOUSE, CIUDAD VICTORIA -- NIGHT   209

The living room couch has been made up with sheets and
blankets. Maria gets ready for bed.

>   SYLVIA
> I can sleep here so you can sleep in
> your room.

>   MARIA
> No, it's ok.

>   SYLVIA
> Can I stay for a while?

Maria nods. Sylvia covers her with the blankets. They look
at each other for a moment. Suddenly Maria points at the
burn on her forearm.

>   MARIA
> What happened?

>   SYLVIA
> Nothing. I burnt myself once.

>   MARIA
> My dad has the same scar in the same
> place.

Sylvia remains silent, looking at her scar.

>   MARIA (CONT'D)
> My dad said he made his scar to never
> forget you.

>   SYLVIA
> So did I.

There is a silence.

>   MARIA
> Are you going to stay with us?

>   SYLVIA
> I don't know, I'd have to talk to
> him. It's been a long time.

>   MARIA
> You're gonna leave again, aren't
> you?

(CONTINUED)

209   CONTINUED: 209

> SYLVIA
> Look...I have to...

Maria just looks at her.

> MARIA
> I'm tired... Good night.

Sylvia and Maria exchange a look.

> SYLVIA
> Good night.

Sylvia switches off the light and makes her way to her room
in the dark.

210   INT. MARIA'S ROOM, CIUDAD VICTORIA -- NIGHT   210

Sylvia walks into the room and looks around: her daughter's
teddy bears, her paintings.

On the wall hang several photographs of Maria and Santiago.
Maria as a baby. Santiago bathing her. Maria, two years
old, next to a dog; seven years old on a bicycle; in a pool
with her friends; eight years old, sitting on Santiago's
lap.

She looks around and suddenly she discovers an old photograph
of herself at seventeen in one of the corners of the mirror.
It is the one that Santiago kept that day at the windmill.
Sylvia looks at it perplexed.

She takes it and sits on the bed. While she looks at it Sylvia
starts to break up.

210A   OMITTED   210A

211   EXT. GINA'S HOUSE -- NIGHT   211

Santiago's truck parks outside Gina's house. Mariana, who's
been waiting, runs out to get in the truck.

212   INT. TRUCK -- NIGHT   212

Santiago opens the door. When Mariana is about to get in,
Pat runs out after her.

> PAT
> Mariana, where are you going?

Mariana ignores him. Pat pulls her by the blouse.

(CONTINUED)

212   CONTINUED: 212

                          PAT (CONT'D)
                What the hell are you doing?

                          MARIANA
                Let me go.

                          PAT
                You can't leave with him.

Mariana pulls away from him, tearing the blouse, and climbs
into the van. Pat tries to stop her from closing the door.

                          PAT (CONT'D)
                I'm going to tell dad.

                          MARIANA
                You tell him whatever you want.

Mariana closes the door and, immediately, Santiago starts
the engine. Pat picks up a rock and throws it at them.

212A   OMITTED   212A

213   EXT. NEW MEXICO DESERT -- DAY   213

The truck is parked on a path in the desert. The sun has
barely risen. Mariana and Santiago are asleep in the cargo
box holding each other. Santiago wakes up and carefully lifts
Mariana's head off his chest and gets up.

He jumps off the back and looks around. Mariana opens her
eyes and sits up.

                          MARIANA
                Where are we?

Santiago points at some mountains.

                          SANTIAGO
                That's Mexico.

Mariana turns and looks at the mass of mountains.

                          MARIANA
                What are we going to do over there.

                          SANTIAGO
                Live in peace.

Mariana thinks for a moment.

                                                        (CONTINUED)

CONTINUED: 213

> MARIANA
> We'll never have peace again.

Santiago walks over to help her get out. He takes one of her hands and she jumps down.

She looks at Mexico again.

> MARIANA (CONT'D)
> I'm pregnant.

> SANTIAGO
> What?

> MARIANA
> I'm pregnant and I don't want it.

Santiago considers Mariana's disclosure.

> SANTIAGO
> We can live in Mexico, the three of us.

> MARIANA
> No, I can't. I can't have it.

214   EXT. HOSPITAL -- DAY   214

The sun barely rises. The Nissan truck is parked outside the hospital. Carlos gets out and closes the door.

214A   INT. NISSAN TRUCK -- DAY   214A

Maria is about to get out but Sylvia holds her arm. Maria turns to her.

> SYLVIA
> I wouldn't have left you if you were a boy.

Maria looks at her, disconcerted.

> MARIA
> What?

> SYLVIA
> I left you because you were a girl. I never could been a girl's mother.

Maria stares at her, silently.

(CONTINUED)

214A   CONTINUED: 214A

> SYLVIA (CONT'D)
> I was afraid you'd come out like me.
> I'm not a good person, you know. I'm
> not. But it hurts me not to have
> seen you grow up.

Sylvia seems hurt while she is talking.

> SYLVIA (CONT'D)
> Maria, forgive me for not being with
> you all these years. Please, forgive
> me.

Maria turns to her.

> MARIA
> I want to see my dad now.

Without another word, she opens the door and walks out,
leaving Sylvia baffled.

215   INT. HALLWAY, HOSPITAL -- DAY   215

Carlos, Maria and Sylvia are sitting in a doctor's office.
Waiting. After a while, the doctor comes in. Both stand up.

> DOCTOR
> Buenos días. [Good morning.]

> CARLOS
> ¿Cómo salió Santiago de la operación?
> [How did the operation go?]

> DOCTOR
> Pudimos drenar y limpiar la infección
> y fusionamos el fémur con clavos.
> [We were able to drain and clean the
> infection, and we fused his femur.]

Maria anxiously interrupts.

> MARIA
> ¿Le cortaron la pierna? [Did you cut
> off his leg?]

> DOCTOR
> No, no perdió la pierna, por ahora
> hija. Tenemos que ver cómo evoluciona.
> Pero por el momento va bien. [No, he
> didn't lose his leg, at least for
> now. We have to check his progress.
> But for the moment, he's doing well.]

(CONTINUED)

215   CONTINUED: 215

Maria turns to Sylvia.

                        MARIA
               The doctor says they didn't cut off
               his leg.

Sylvia smiles at her. Maria turns to the doctor.

                   MARIA (CONT'D)
               ¿Puedo verlo? [Can I see him?]

                        DOCTOR
               Sí, pueden verlo, pero todavía se
               está recuperando de la anestesia.
               [Yes, you can see him, but he's still
               recovering from the anesthetic.]

Maria runs toward the room.

216   EXT. HALLWAY, HOSPITAL -- DAY   216

Sylvia watches her walk down the hallway. Maria stops, turns
and fixes her eyes on her. Their eyes meet.

                        MARIA
               Are you coming?

217   EXT. GINA'S HOUSE -- MORNING   217

The person who is looking now is Gina, who is leaving her
house. She looks both ways and heads toward her car.

She opens the door of her Pinto to get in.

218   INT. SANTIAGO'S CAR -- MORNING   218

It is Santiago (17) who gets into his truck. He starts the
engine and drives off. Through the window Santiago sees
Mariana standing with her bike in the desert.

219   EXT. NEW MEXICO DESERT -- MORNING   219

The car pulling away belongs to Nick, who drives toward the
trailer home in the distance. On the steps to the trailer we
can see Gina waiting for him.

Nick parks. He opens the door to get out and walks to her.

220   EXT. SORGHUM FIELDS -- MORNING   220

Walking through the sorghum fields is Carlos. A plane flies
overhead and descends to fumigate the sorghum fields.

                                              (CONTINUED)

220   CONTINUED: 220

　　　Carlos watches it fly past and keeps walking.

221   EXT. HOUSE, TAMAULIPAS -- MORNING   221

　　　It is Maria who is walking now, down a sidewalk in Ciudad
　　　Victoria, toward her house. She opens the door.

222   INT. HOUSE, TAMAULIPAS -- DAY   222

　　　She enters and walks toward the living room. In a wheelchair,
　　　with his leg bandaged is Santiago (30) who smiles when he
　　　sees her. She hurries to go give him a kiss.

223   INT. TRAILER HOME -- MORNING   223

　　　It is Nick and Gina who are kissing. They pull away. She
　　　gets up and opens the curtains.

224   INT. SYLVIA'S APARTMENT -- MORNING   224

　　　Sylvia is opening her curtains, with the sea in the distance.
　　　She turns toward her room.

225   INT. ROOM MEXICAN TOWN -- MORNING   225

　　　In the room, in a humble house, Santiago (16) is asleep with
　　　a crib next to him. Mariana sits down in the bed and kisses
　　　him tenderly, stroking his head.

　　　She stands up, goes to a crib and looks at Maria, just born.
　　　She leans over to kiss her, and then watches her for a long
　　　time. She starts to cry quietly.

　　　She turns around, picks up a box tied with string that
　　　contains her belongings, and goes to open the door.

226   EXT. TOWN, MEXICO -- DAY   226

　　　She opens the door to a northern Mexican town. The streets
　　　are empty; just one local can be seen out walking.

　　　Mariana sighs and starts walking. After a few steps she stops
　　　and looks back.

227   INT. HOSPITAL -- DAY   227

　　　Sylvia looks ahead. Her eyes meet with Maria who waits for
　　　her in the hall. She breathes deeply and walks toward her.

                          T H E   E N D

Las Cruces, New Mexico-Mexico City- Los Angeles, October 17,
2007.

PRODUCTION NOTES

Author and screenwriter Guillermo Arriaga believes that you can't simply sit down and write a story: "You have to wait until the story is mature enough to be told," he says when explaining that the idea for his screenplay *The Burning Plain* evolved over almost fifteen years before he began putting it down on paper in 2005. The multi-narrative drama where the seemingly unconnected past and present eventually intersect continues a signature style that garnered him critical acclaim and worldwide commercial success for his screenplays for the films *Babel, 21 Grams, The Three Burials of Melquiades Estrada,* and *Amores Perros.*

To help him bring his vision to the screen, Arriaga approached what at first seemed like unlikely auspices for the project: producers Walter Parkes and Laurie MacDonald, who in the past have been known for producing big studio-based movies which have found both critical and commercial success, such as *Men In Black, Gladiator,* and *Sweeney Todd.*

"It's not hyperbole to say that Guillermo has pretty much invented a new way of telling motion picture stories," says Parkes. "What particularly excited us here, beyond the evocation of the "four elements" as the basis of a script, was the fact that Guillermo wanted to use his unique structural approach to unravel and elucidate the emotional mystery of a central character—Sylvia, who is in really the lynchpin of the entire story, and who we knew would attract a great actress."

Adds MacDonald: "It was both a creative opportunity and a challenge to work with an artist of Guillermo's stature. The normal rules of screenplay development really don't apply—but what surprised us was how open and collaborative he was in the process, despite the fact that the story is such a personal one. We didn't know it at the time but it would bode very well for Guillermo's ability to direct his movie."

It wasn't until after submitting the screenplay to Parkes and MacDonald, and executive producer Alisa Tager, that Arriaga expressed interest in directing. "In some ways, it was a very easy decision to support Guillermo as the director of the movie. His approach to the material is so singular, so personal, and so specific that it is hard to imagine someone else interpreting it," says Parkes, "The movie existed fully on the page." Adds MacDonald: "There's also an inherent excitement in supporting a first-time director, particularly if he has already proven himself as a creator of original material."

At this point, Todd Wagner and Mark Cuban's 2929 Productions came on board to finance. 2929 President and executive producer Marc Butan cites the rich characters, the cinematic backdrop, and Arriaga's unique storytelling style as his main attractions to the script: "This is not a classically structured movie and audiences will have to figure it out on their own, as it unfolds on the screen," said Butan. But Arriaga disputes the notion that his style is unconventional or unique: "If I want to tell you how I grew up in Mexico maybe I will start with my grandfather who came from a remote state in the south, and then go to my son because my son looks like my father, and then I'm telling that story. This is natural for people, even if cinema hasn't always approached storytelling that way," asserts Arriaga.

On Arriaga's first time behind the camera, Butan notes, "a big part of the decision is whether this is a person who can inspire and command loyalty among a group of people for a period of time." Arriaga's material belies his presence on set. Says executive producer Ray Angelic, "He writes these dark, emotional, oftentimes tragic stories and when you meet him he's one of the warmest, most lovable guys I've ever seen on set," as he recalls Arriaga's daily interaction with the cast and crew. Butan calls Arriaga "a very straightforward person," whose richly detailed scripts "are his vision for the movie." So there were very few surprises from Arriaga, both as a person and from his goals as a filmmaker. And because Arriaga was very actively involved in the productions of his previous scripts, 2929 didn't consider him "a writer who had been sitting at home writing and all of a sudden wants to direct," says Butan.

• • •

With 2929 committed to making his film, Arriaga needed to find his cast. To play Sylvia, a beautiful but scarred woman hiding from her past, Arriaga knew he needed an actress who would be able to convey a deep interior trauma but who also would be compelling to audiences. Charlize Theron, who had won an Oscar for her portrayal of a woman damaged by a traumatic youth in *Monster*, was the obvious choice. Arriaga approached their one-hour lunch meeting with trepidation. But as the meeting stretched to five hours and the conversation deepened, Arriaga realized he had his Sylvia. "When Charlize said yes, that really helped to make this film possible," concluded Arriaga.

Theron was haunted by the story after her first read through the script. "I found myself thinking about it nonstop and that's always a good sign," says Theron. "This story and the other characters in the film force Sylvia into a corner," continues Theron, who saw in her character parallels with her personal convictions about the human condition. "You get to a place in your life where you have to step up and face your demons, face your reality. That's the difference between us and every other animal: we can overcome our initial instinct to protect ourselves from pain." Of Sylvia, Theron says, "She's not naturally the kind of person to look into the mirror and say, 'Okay these are things that you have to deal with.' But by the end of the film, that's where she has to be."

"From our first meeting I realized that we collaborated really well and that we were definitely on the same page with the character," recalls Theron, who also joined the production in the role of executive producer. "I have to feel that I'm going to have a clear partnership with my director and that there's going to be a constant dialogue and communication," says Theron. That's the only way she'd be able to "really get to the bottom line of the character and what the story is about." The relationship between actor and director immediately took root as Theron and Arriaga talked and sent text messages continually before she arrived on location in New Mexico, her character's childhood home.

The feeling of partnership was mutual and Arriaga appreciated the early dialogue that he developed with Theron. "The character's journey is very painful," explains Arriaga when reflecting on Charlize's subtle, minimalist approach to Sylvia's troubled past. "Charlize did it without simplifying it because this kind of material can easily become melodramatic or stylized." Theron felt Arriaga's way of telling her character's story was very original in that it shows the audience Sylvia's pain long before giving it context. Says Theron, "It gives you the feeling of dislocation, like the pain has become something separate from the event that caused it. That's what Sylvia's experiencing and that's also what the audience is experiencing." And because she's been suppressing her emotions for so long, Sylvia's expression of these emotions during the course of the story would necessarily be small and telling, rather than explosive and dramatic.

Though 2929's Butan concedes that there was a very short list of actresses considered for the role of Gina, the idea came from Theron, wearing her executive producer hat. The role is a delicate one—a married woman and mother of four children who has a passionate affair with a married man from a different background. The only way for the film to work was to get the audience

113

invested in this extramarital affair—the event that causes the cascade of both trauma and redemption. Arriaga found in Basinger's work to possess "a kind of fragility that suited the character very well." On working with Basinger, Arriaga says, "Kim trusted me, which is very important in the relationship between actor and director." For Arriaga she embodied "this contradiction between what is going on in the mind and the heart. These contradictions are so hard to show but Kim did it."

• • •

The Burning Plain was shot over eight weeks on location in the Chihuahuan Desert region of New Mexico and the brooding coastal region of Oregon inland to Portland. Not only were the two regions presented as full-fledged characters in the story, but Arriaga feels that their dominant elements represented events and emotions in his characters' lives. "It's part of the storytelling so I was very careful with how the landscape was portrayed," says Arriaga.

"We scouted the entire state of New Mexico with three or four separate scouts," says executive producer Ray Angelic. "Guillermo really responded to Las Cruces in particular and specifically to the Organ Mountains. Each time we went back he spent more time in Las Cruces and really felt that was the place." The completely unobstructed stretch of land along the foot of that mountain range provided the perfect sense of vastness and isolation for the love affair between two of the film's main characters.

• • •

For his ensemble of talent, Arriaga wanted actors who would convey the sense of reality that is so elemental to telling his story. To that end, casting director Debra Zane, who cast ensemble dramas like *American Beauty, Seabiscuit,* and *Traffic*, scoured both the southwestern US and Mexico for actors who could lend this earthy quality to the story. Arriaga describes working with Zane as "a very intense and beautiful process. She has impeccable taste and was like a rock in the construction of the film."

Citing Theron as her inspiration for becoming an actress, Jennifer Lawrence got the part of Mariana, the impulsive adolescent reeling from the death of her mother but still oblivious to the consequences of her actions. "After I finished reading, Guillermo came over and kissed me on the forehead," recalls Lawrence. "Debra asked me if I wanted to see anybody else for Mariana," reiterated Arriaga, "and I said 'Nope! This is the one!'"

Lawrence, who plays a teenager confused and burdened by a mother's rejection of the family after surviving a bout with cancer, displayed an internal intensity during the casting that Arriaga sought for Mariana. "When you first meet my character she's been the *de facto* mother of her siblings for the past four years and hasn't had a chance to be a kid," explains Lawrence. It's that resentment, says Lawrence, "that really drives the story for the rest of the characters." During shooting, Lawrence maintained that separation off-screen, avoiding her character's mother, Basinger. It was a relief to Lawrence, however, when the two enjoyed a hug at the end of filming.

At seventeen, Lawrence's age belies her maturity as an actor and Arriaga found that she had the same kind of commitment to the film as Theron. "They're both willing to do anything on behalf of the character," acknowledged Arriaga. "I had two Charlizes on this film!"

J. D. Pardo, who plays young Santiago, the teenaged boy whose family has been torn apart by the revelation of his father's death and infidelity, needed to have a certain tragic chemistry with Lawrence. "A lot of the weight of the film is in the story between Santiago and Mariana," elaborates Arriaga. "They both have undergone similar traumas but handle it in different ways—for that reason they find each other mysterious. There was a lot of this same weighty chemistry between J. D. and Jennifer and I had no doubt that they would do it right."

For Pardo this "true growing-up story" provided all the nuances of what young men go though when trying to get close to their fathers. "You're asking yourself questions about who your father was and you're searching…and this really hit home," says Pardo of his hopeful take on Santiago's heartbreaking loss of his father.

Arriaga insisted on bringing in Jose Maria Yazpik from Mexico to play Carlos, the older Santiago's best friend and partner in a crop-dusting business. "Guillermo was very passionate about Jose Maria in that role," said Butan, who acknowledged that there were several high profile Mexican-American actors interested in it. Arriaga met Yazpik ten years ago after viewing a short film a student showed him featuring the actor. "I was mesmerized by this actor and told him that I wanted to work together some day," recalls Arriaga.

To prepare him for the role, Yazpik explains that Arriaga "told me stories about his friend Melquiades Estrada. He really exists and he based this film's character upon Melquiades' sort of bipolar personality, very happy in one instant and then the next he will just not speak." Yazpik believes this "Arriaga-esque" love story honors not only the feelings between lovers but also the love between friends, and the love between parents and children. "Carlos is not happy about his friend's situation or the changes it could engender, but will endure the stark 'fish out of water' journey required to make things right again."

The story takes emotional hairpin turns, often without dialogue. Arriaga admired the actor's pitch perfect portrayal of Carlos and says, "in Jose Maria's performance we see this man whose innocence and loyalty to his friend is palpable. He pulled Carlos exactly to where I wanted him to be."

Danny Pino, who plays Carlos' best friend, the older Santiago, "brought the character some lightness," says Arriaga. "He had this kind of hope to his performance, and in this film we needed someone that would represent a guy who has worked his way up in life and makes it even with difficult circumstances: He's lost the love of his life but manages to find hope and take comfort in the fact that he has her daughter." Similarly, Pino finds that the story evokes forgiveness and second chances. "Santiago has managed to raise his daughter with the help of his best friend, but has an obstacle that forces him to reach out to the estranged mother of his daughter," explains Pino. He was drawn to the story's complex but very real characters. "That's part of the genius of what Guillermo has been able to accomplish," says Pino of Arriaga's script. "He's been able to give you a true taste of what these people's lives are like."

When a serious injury forces Santiago to send his friend, Carlos, to track down Maria's mother, all of the pain of Maria's estrangement from her mother comes to the surface. On finding his Maria, Arriaga says, "I really put a gun to my own head when I wrote the script. Not only did I need a girl who speaks perfect English and perfect Spanish, but she had to be beautiful enough to be the daughter of a Mexican man and a blond-haired blue-eyed woman!" After endless casting sessions in LA and New York, Arriaga and casting director Debra Zane spread the word in Mexico. A tape of Tessa Ia made its way to the casting office. She met all the physical and language criteria, so she flew to LA to meet with Arriaga. "During the casting session I saw that she had a fierce glance when she looks at you, so I hired her" says Arriaga.

"Maria has never had a mother and is used to living only with her Dad," says Ia of her character. "She thinks it's monstrous for someone to leave a baby. But she's also the only one who can put everyone beyond the pain their past." In working through the delicate reunion scenes between Maria and her mother, Ia recalls "Maria is afraid to get close when she meets her because she might leave again, but afterwards she lets her come to her world."

• • •

Just as Basinger embodied Gina, Arriaga felt so strongly that Brett Cullen was the only actor who could play her husband Robert—in fact, that he ran after the actor to tell him he'd gotten the part. "When he auditioned he began talking about his own family and I saw something deep inside this guy," remembers Arriaga. In talking about his character, Arriaga asked Cullen something that was very difficult for him to answer. "I asked him if Robert knows how to swim, and he said yes," recalls Arriaga. "Then I asked him 'Where, living in the desert, did Robert learn to swim?' and he replied that he needed to think about his answers. So he wrote a beautiful story about his character and he sent it to me. This is something I will be thankful for the rest of my life." For Cullen, Robert embodied the universal 'shattered man' who he says "has been through a very tough period of time with his family and I think it puts in question his belief in himself, his belief maybe somewhat in God."

Nick, the Mexican–American whom Gina falls in love with, was another difficult character for Arriaga to cast. He had to be someone who still looks and feels Mexican. "We looked at many very fine actors but the problem wasn't whether they were good actors," said Arriaga, "the difficulty was the chemistry between him and Kim Basinger. We were running out of options when we finally got to Joaquim, who is not Mexican—he's Portuguese. But it was one of these lucky moments when the gods looked down and said, 'Hey, here's this guy for you.' Joaquim is a man who looks virile, who looks like he belongs in the land-scape and I think he has a sexiness, which made me feel this married woman could be in love with him." The role is complicated by the fact that, unlike with Gina, the film would never reveal Nick's backstory. The depth of their passion would have to be implied through performance rather than exposition. "I wanted the audience not to know how they met, just as Mariana and Santiago don't know how their parents met—I just wanted the audience to feel the connection between Nick and Gina, obscure but powerful."

• • •

"I only write of things I know and things that have touched me per-sonally," says Arriaga who would use his own life and stories when discussing an upcoming scene with actors. "He had a very clear vision of the whole movie in his head," confirms Angelic. "He knows what each character is wearing, where they live and what kind of car they drive. He was great with the cast."

At their first meeting Arriaga told Angelic that he was looking to cre-ate a real feeling of family and team spirit with the cast and crew, and that they would come onboard because they were passionate about the material.

From their time together preparing the film Angelic was very aware of Arriaga's strength as a screenwriter, so the focus of his work was "a matter of surrounding him with creative department heads who could really support, guide and help him in obtaining his vision."

"One of my luckiest choices in this film was hiring Robert Elswit who was not only my director of photography, but would become my teacher," says Arriaga. "He taught me many things on this film and I will always be thankful to him. When he came to my office to talk about this film, he only talked about the story. He never talked about lenses or camera equipment or technical things, he just talked about the story, which really impressed me."

"Robert's such a hard worker and accepted this film already being committed to another film with a slight schedule conflict, so the last part of the picture was photographed by John Toll," explains Arriaga. "The film is basically four stories and Robert shot three of them and John Toll shot one of them with the help and preparation of Robert, and I think that having two of the greatest DPs in history was a luxury that not every director is privileged to have."

Elswit actually brought up the idea of having a different DP do the Portland portion of the film explains Angelic, "and going from one great DP to another made sense to the story too. Oregon is a completely separate story line with a completely different look and different geography from the rest of the film. Elswit and Toll are friends and when we found out that John was interested and excited by it then we became interested and excited about the idea of switching DPs."

Production designer Dan Leigh cites the time/space continuum that Arriaga toys with in this story as "a puzzle that makes an audience participate in watching a film." He was drawn to the challenge of visually helping an audience solve the puzzle, and in his first meeting with Arriaga learned that the original title was "The Elements," for the medieval concepts of earth-air-fire-water. These elements, and using the film's locations to emphasize the elemental quality of the story, were a major focus of their first discussion.

"Guillermo identifies certain characters with each of those elements," said Leigh, so a seamless color pallet between the outside colors and the interiors established that nature force of the characters' environments whether the earth and air of the desert or the sea and rain of the Pacific coast. One of the most striking uses of color in is the vast red plain of sorghum fields. "Guillermo has always said that one of his feelings about screenwriting is to always bear in mind that you want to show your audience something that they haven't seen… and I can't think of a time that sorghum has ever been seen in a movie."

"Dan Leigh was the gatekeeper of my visions," affirms Arriaga. "If he had any doubts about the suitability of a location, he was the first to say that it was not what we were looking for. He helped me keep my vision in mind and he was very much into the storytelling."

Costume designer Cindy Evans was also an important element to the film. Arriaga says, "Cindy brought a sense of reality and storytelling to the characters, adding personality and emotion. Directing the actors was made easier by the sensible work of Cindy, who helped define the characters through their costumes. Going to Cindy's workplace was like going to an oasis. Every one was relaxed, happy and working extremely hard."

Producers Walter Parkes and Laurie MacDonald recommended editor Craig Wood and Arriaga was impressed with his previous work. "He and I have a great connection and he has a sense of the pace and of the characters," reflects Arriaga who began the editing process with Wood while shooting in New Mexico. "His attention is focused on cuts that will help the character development and he tends to keep the scenes as long as possible and doesn't feel the need to cut and cut and cut." Because of the unconventional narrative structure, Wood needed to the scenes to play out elementally, with long takes and traditional cutting styles. "There is a certain geometry to the way Craig cuts," says Arriaga, "He orients you so quickly that, even if it can be jarring to go from Portland to Las Cruces, he makes you feel as though you are gently entering a new world, like all the worlds are connected—which they are."

It was extremely gratifying for Arriaga to go from the solitary life of a writer to actually interacting with characters he created. "After being so lonely, writing so many years, it was the ultimate pleasure being in the desert and beautiful landscapes in Oregon with all these wonderful friends working along so hard with me," says Arriaga. "It was very tough—all movies are—but I felt on this set everyone was a filmmaker," says Arriaga, "and for the first time I say to everyone this is not my film; this is our film."

For Arriaga, that, ultimately, is the paradox of filmmaking: "It's something that is so difficult and yet people love the process so much." But it's also the paradox of *The Burning Plain*'s story. Says Arriaga, "How does something as beautiful as two people making love cause such an obstacle for love in other characters? That is one of the great romantic mysteries and just to able to explore it even a little bit through cinema is a gift I'll never forget."

CAST AND CREW CREDITS

2929 PRODUCTIONS PRESENTS
IN ASSOCIATION WITH COSTA FILMS
A PARKES + MACDONALD PRODUCTION
CHARLIZE THERON   KIM BASINGER

"THE BURNING PLAIN"

JOHN CORBETT   JOAQUIM DE ALMEIDA   DANNY PINO

casting by
DEBRA ZANE, C.S.A.

costume Designer
CINDY EVANS

music supervisors
DANA SANO AND
ANNETTE FRADERA

music by
OMAR RODRIGUEZ LOPEZ
& HANS ZIMMER

editor
CRAIG WOOD

production designer
DAN LEIGH

director of photography
ROBERT ELSWIT, A.S.C.

co-producers
BETH KONO EDUARDO
COSTANTINI MIKE UPTON

executive producers
CHARLIZE THERON ALISA
TAGER RAY ANGELIC

executive producers
TODD WAGNER MARK
CUBAN MARC BUTAN

produced by
WALTER PARKES AND
LAURIE MACDONALD

written and directed by
GUILLERMO ARRIAGA

translation by
ALAN PAGE

CAST
(In order of appearance)

Sylvia . . . . Charlize Theron
John . . . . John Corbett
Carlos . . . . Jose Maria Yazpik
Laura . . . . Robin Tunney
Lawrence . . . . Gray Eubank
Sophie . . . . Fernanda Romero
Vivi . . . . Kacie Thomas
Young Man . . . . Martin Papazian
Cook . . . . Sean McGrath
Young Santiago . . . . J D Pardo
Cristobal . . . . Diego Torres
Xavier . . . . José Gallardo, Jr.
Ana . . . . Rachel Ticotin
Aunt Rebecca . . . . Rosalia De Aragon
Paula . . . . Debrianna Mansini
Priest . . . . Anthony Escobar
Robert . . . . Brett Cullen
Mariana . . . . Jennifer Lawrence
Pat . . . . T J Plunket
Bobby . . . . Taylor Warden
Monnie . . . . Stacy Marie Warden
Santiago . . . . Danny Pino
Operator . . . . Aidé Rodriquez
Maria . . . . Tessa Ia

Woman . . . . Toni Lopez
Rancher #1 . . . . Luis Senyé
Rancher #2 . . . . Kirk Zachek
Nick Martinez . . . . Joaquim De Almeida
Gina . . . . Kim Basinger
Pat's Friend . . . . Kyle Klunder
Doctor . . . . Rafael Hernández
Nurse . . . . Kimberlynn Guzman

Stunt Coordinators . . . . Brian Smyj
                                  Peewee Piemonte
Pilot/ Aerial Coordinator . . . Peter J. McKernan
Pilot/Stunts . . . . Howard Isreal
Stunts . . . . Shauna Duggins
                                  Tyra Dillenschneider

For
Maru, Mariana y Santiago
Con todo y para siempre

PRODUCTION

Unit Production Manager . . . . . . Ray Angelic
First Assistant Director . . . . Phil Hardage
Second Assistant Director . . . . . Keith W. Potter
Additional Photography . . . . . John Toll, A.S.C.
Production Supervisor . . . . Marjorie Ergas

Associate Producer . . . . Adrián Zurita
Art Director . . . . Naython Vane
Set Decorators. . . Wil Pfau, Ron Von Blomberg
First Assistant Editor. . . . . . . Simon Morgan
Post Production Supervisor . . . . . Jamey Pryde
2929 Senior Vice President of Post Production
. . . . Marc Wuertemburg
"A" Camera 1st Assistant . . . . . . Baz Idoine
"A" Camera 2nd Assistant. . . . . Larissa Supplitt
Steadicam Operator/ "B" Camera Operator
. . . . Scott Sakamoto
"B" Camera 1st Assistant. . . . . . James Apted
Peter Geraghty, Ray Milazzo, Jr.
"B" Camera 2nd Assistant. . . . Tom Hutchinson
Kevin Huver
2nd Unit DP/ "C" Camera Operator
. . . . Heather Page
"C" Camera 1st Assistant . . . . . Penny Sprague
"D" Camera 1st Assistant . . . Christopher Mack
Camera Loader. . . . . Kelly Simpson
Remote Camera Technician. . . . . . Joe Datri
Stills Photographer . . . . . . Richard Foreman
Video Assist . . . . Jeremiah Chapman
24 Frame Playback . . . . Frank Eyers
Script Supervisor. . . . . . . Brooke Satrazemis
Production Sound Mixer . . . Lori Dovi, C.A.S.
Boom Operator . . . . David Allen Smith
Utility Sound . . . . Thadd Day
Chief Lighting Technician . . . . . Rick Thomas
Assistant Chief Lighting Tech. . . Dante Cardone
Electricians. . . . . Joe Bacharka
Theo Bott
John Joleaud
Rob Locker
Karina Teismann
Kevin Wisor
Additional Electrician. . . . . . Joseph J. Sikora
Rigging Gaffer . . . . Jeff Stewart
Best Boy Rigging Electrician . . . . Tor Matson
Rigging Electricians . . . . . . Dominic Pagano
Steve Reed
Key Grip . . . . Michael Kenner
Best Boy Grip . . . . Johnny Morris
Dolly Grip. . . . . Jeff Kunkel
Grips . . . . Gary Christie
Juergen Heinemann
Kaleb Heinemann
Amber Maahs
Guillermo A. Partillo III
Additional Grips. . . Danielle "Stella" Hernandez
Daniel Miller
Dan Williams
Aerial DP/2nd Unit Director . . . . Dylan Goss
Spacecam Technician. . . . . Vahagn Gharibyan

Special Effects Coordinator . . . . David Fletcher
Special Effects Foreman . . . . Tom Kittle
Special Effects Technicians. . . . Vincent Lee Ball
William Catania
James "J.C." Cheshire
Gregory Oliver
Art Department Coordinator/Additional Graphics
. . . . Vicki McWilliams
Art Department Production Assistant
. . . . Robin Scala
Leadperson. . . . . Severino Gonzales
On Set Dresser. . . . . Lisa Corradino
Gang Boss . . . . Christopher Painter
Set Dressers. . . . . Michael Myszka
Robert Jackson
Spencer Stair
Additional Set Dressers . . . . Ra Arancio-Parrain
John A. Gutierrez
Peter Pinon III
Gabriel Rivera
Set Decorator Production Assistant
. . . . Sheila Griffin
Set Decorating Intern . . . . Sara Corral
Storyboard Artists . . . . Chris Buchinsky
Joseph Guillette
Property Master . . . . Joe Arnold
Assistant Property Master . . . . . Josiah O'Neil
Construction Coordinators . . . . . Noah Bradley
Dennis W. Garland
Foreman . . . . Mike Daigle
Gang Boss . . . . Jim Gill
Propmakers . . . . Arthur Arndt
Stephen Braddock
Lance Tytor
Lead Scenic Painter . . . . . . Kenneth Pattison
Scenic Painters . . . . Anna Cosentine
Gabriel Flores
William Maloney
Christina Pizzala
Utility Technicians . . . . Kevin Brown
Ralph DeLaurentis
Janice B. Jacobson
Key Greens . . . . Dennis W. Garland
Greens . . . . Ben Bishop, Ray Mark Provencio
Assistant Costume Designer. . . . . Lisa Parmet
Costume Supervisor . . . . Barcie Waite
Costumer to Ms. Theron . Annie Laoparadonchai
Costumer to Ms. Basinger . . . Cynthia Summer
Key Set Costumer. . . . . John Deering
Set Costumer . . . . Juliet Hyde-White
Additional Set Costumer . . . . . Dionne Barens
Seamstress . . . . Deborah Andrews
Costume Production Assistant . . . . . Lisa Clark
Department Head Hair Stylist. . Ramona Fleetwood

Key Hair Stylist . . . . Yvette Meely
Hair Stylist to Ms. Basinger . . . . . Mitch Stone
Additional Hair Stylist . . . . . Reyna Robinson
Department Head Make-Up Artist . . Sara Bozik
Key Make-Up Artist. . . . Sheila Trujillo-Gomez
Make-Up Artist to Ms. Basinger . June Brickman
Body Make-Up Artist to Ms. Basinger
. . . . Jane English
Additional Make-Up Artist. . . . . Lisa Hill
Prosthetic Provider . . . . Matthew Mungle
Production Accountant . . . . . Cyndy Fujikawa
First Assistant Accountant . . . . . Jennifer Cobb
Payroll Accountants . . . . Laura Fearon
Estrella Perez
Accounting Clerks. . . . . Bernadette Valer
Mark Ver Ploegh
Post Production Accountant. . . . . . Tracy Nash
Production Office Coordinator . . Shanti Delsarte
Assistant Production Office Coordinator
. . . . Marissa Gonzales
Production Secretary . . . . Elias Vigil
Travel Coordinators . . . . . . Cherron Kofford
Jill Vaupen
Production Office Assistant . . . . . Jesse Terry
Production Office Interns . . . . Rachel Bailey
Leandra M. Barreras
Sean Dolan
Alison Marwah
Matt Wilson
Assistant to Mr. Arriaga. . . David Barraza Ibanez
Micaela Maestas
Assistant to Mr. Parks & Ms. MacDonald
. . . . Riyoko Tanaka
Assistant to Ms. Theron. . . . . . . Ashlee Irish
Assistant to Mr. Butan . . . . Jeff Zaks
Assistant to Ms Tager . . . . Tonia Davis
Assistant to Mr. Angelic . . . . Ilana Lapid
Assistant to Mr. Wagner. . . . . . Staci Mitchell
Assistant to Mr. Cuban . . . . Dawn Knox
Assistant to Ms. Kono . . . . Bryon Schreckengost
Script Translator. . . . . Alan Page
2nd Second Assistant Director . . . . Chad Saxton
Addtional First Assistant Directors. . . Thomas G.
Parris, Matthew D. Smith
Key Production Assistant . . . . Emily Gruendike
Set Production Assistants . . . . . . Matt Freeman
Sue Foley
Paul Gladden
Brian Green
Ari Joffe
Mary McGinn
John Paul Potter
Jaron Whitfill
Location Manager . . . . Jean Chien

Assistant Location Managers . . . Santino Jimenez
Roderick Peyketewa
2nd Assistant Location Manager . Aimée Schaefer
Location Productions Assistants . . . . Levi Smith
Kaleb Wentzel-Fisher
Aerial Location Scout . . . . Eric Papa
Location Intern. . . . . Jared Ortega
Set Medic . . . . Jim Ivy
Casting Associate . . . . Tannis Vallely
Casting Assistant . . . . Shayna Markowitz
New Mexico Casting. . . . . Kathy Brink
New Mexico Casting Assistant . . Aaron Giomolini
Extras Casting . . . . Fernando Echeverri
Lexington Hoebel
Extras Casting Assistant . . . . . . Julie Rounds
Studio Teachers. . . . . Kathleen Brenton-Collier
Dia Hahn
On-Set Tutor . . . . Murielle Helgeson
Marketing Consultant . . . . Diane Slattery
Animals Provided by . . . . . The Animal Agency
Animal Trainers. . . . . Trevor Fowler
Transportation Captains. . . . . Billy Getzwiller
Prentis "PW" Woods"
Picture Car Coordinator. . . . . . . Jacob Cena
Drivers. . . . . Dan Berryman
Tom Berto
David Burke
Jim Christian
Earl Scott Corley
Felix Delgado
Tyra Dillenschneider
James Everett
Paul M. Hackett
Kenny James
Fritz Kaser
Robert J. Kozlowski
Gavin Lebow
Belarmino A. Bill Lopez
Jimmy W. Masterson
Eric Miller
R. Daniel Miller
Tom Perkins
Ken Plumlee
Robert M. "Billy" Rabelo
Teri Romano
Marlin "Boots" Southerland
Glen Stalcup
Andrew Trujillo
Matt Wagner
Paul Walker
Byron Wilkerson
Leanne Wilkerson
William Wray
Catering Provided by . . Alex's Gourmet Catering

Chef. . . . . Luis Montenegro
Assistant Chefs . . . . Teodoro Benitez
Nestor "Noe" Lopez

Craft Services . . . . Patricia Perkins

PORTLAND UNIT

Production Supervisor . . . . . . Darren Demetre
"B" Camera 2nd Assistant . . . . Nate Goodman
Chief Lighting Technician. . . . . Jarred Waldron
Rigging Gaffers . . . . Mathew D. May
Scott Walters
Electricians . . . . Andy Barden
Chris "Chalky" Chalk
James R. Davis
Ryan Middleton
Stephen Purcell
Jean Margaret Thomas
Grips. . . . . Chip Ingram
Brent Lawson
Brian Lawson
Bruce Lawson
Joe Vitellaro
Utility Sound. . . . . Eric Goldstein
Video Assist . . . . Gaylen Nebeker
24 Frame Playback. . . . . Martin Wright
Art Directors . . . . Jim Donahue
Ben Hayden
Art Department Coordinator . . . . . Alex Klaue
Storyboard Artist . . . . Dan Schaefer
Construction Coordinator. . . . . Randal Groves
Construction Foremen . . . . . . Daas Bersana
Johnny Trudell
Lead Scenic/Stand by Painter. . . . Renee Prince
Additional Scenics. . . . . Ken Erck
Bree Judah
Greens. . . . . Charlie Carlsen
Prop Makers . . . . Brad Anderson
David J. Rivers
Prop Assistant . . . . Carly Sertic
Set Decorator. . . . . Sean Kennedy
Leadman . . . . Sean Fong
On-Set Dresser . . . . Ryan Smith
Buyer. . . . . Teresa J. Tamiyasu
Set Dressers . . . . Philip Blackburn
Jenelle Giordano
Adam Johnson
Bekka Melino
Chandler Vinar
Key Set Costumer . . . . Nikki Paulson-Bartnick
Set Costumer . . . . Chapin Simpson
Additional Costumer. . . . . Lis Bothwell
Additional Make-Up . . . . Crystal Shade
Production Coordinator . . . . . Wendy Kutzner

Assistant Office Production Coordinator
. . . . Wilson Peery
Production Secretary . . . . Stephani Norwood
Office Production Assistants
. . . . Aimee Lynn Barneburg
Crystal Walen
Payroll Accountant . . . . . Gabriel DellaVecchia
Accounting Clerk. . . . . Colleen Martinez
Location Manager. . . . . Doug Hobart
Assistant Location Manager. . . . Bobby Warberg
2nd Assistant Location . . . . . . Tracy Holliday
Location Production Assistant . . . Andrew Ticer
Set Production Assistants . . . . . Jackson Rowe
Derek Wilson
Aimee Schaefer
Ari Joffe
Portland Casting . . . . Lana Veenker, C.S.A.
Portland Casting Associate . . . . . . Lori Lewis
Portland Casting Assistant. . . . . Eryn Goodman
Portland Casting Administrative Assistant
. . . . Haley Talbot
Portland Extra Casting
. . . . Rutabaga Background Casting
Extra Casting . . . . Diana Hammons
Extras Casting Assistant . . . . . Diane Kerstein
Catering Assistants . . . . Pedro Delgadillo
Angel Estrada
Craft Services . . . . Brittnee DeWald
David Wiliams
Lead Medic . . . . Taylor Saxon
Rigging Medic . . . . Karla Benson
Special Effects Coordinator. . . . . Robert Riggs
Additional Special Effects . . Stephen Klineburger
Studio Teacher Coordinator . Morag MacPherson
On-Set Tutor . . . . Murielle Helgeson
Transportation Captains . . . . Eric Miller
David Norris

Drivers. . . . . Mischa Austreng
Steve Evans
Ryder Greene
Mark Haleston
Bart Heimburger
Lance Hruza
Philip Krysl
Brendan McKeon
Greg McVey
Andrew Mott
John "JP" Petty
Robert Platt
Thomas Platt
Joe Solberg
Eric Somonson
Laura Stride
Don Williams

POST PRODUCTION

Sound Editorial Services by . . . . . Soundeluxe
Supervising Sound Editor. . . . . Mike Wilhoit
Sound Designers . . . . Scott Wolf
Karen Vassar
Dialogue Editor . . . . . . Laura Harris Atkinson
Foley Editor . . . . Michael Hertlein
Assistant Sound Editor . . . . . Paul Flinchbaugh
Re-recording Services by Universal Studios Sound
Re-recording Mixers . . . . Jon Taylor
Christian P. Minkler
Recordist. . . . . Unsun Song
Stage Engineer . . . . Jack Snyder
Foley by . . . Paramount Post Production Services
Foley Artists. . . . . Robin Harlan
Sarah Monat
Foley Mixer. . . . . Randy Singer
ADR Mixers . . . . Doc Kane
Ron Bedrosian
ADR Recordists . . . . . . Jeannette Browning
Julio Carmona
Audio Restoration. . . . . Lars Bjerre
Voice Casting by . . . . The Final Word
Loop Group Voices . . . . Richard Cansino
Joe Cappelletti
Greg Ellis
Kate Higgins
Alejandra Gollas
Mike Gomez
Lex Lang
Sal Lopez
Dyana Ortelli
Jacqueline Piñol
Cindy Robinson
Digital Intermediate Provided by . . Company 3
Co3 Executive Producer . . . . Stefan Sonnenfeld
Digital Intermediate Colorist . Stephen Nakamura
Digital Intermediate Producer . . . . . Des Carey
On-Line Editor. . . . . Alex Romano
DI Technologist . . . . Mike Chiado
DI Scanning Supervisor . . . . . Michael Boggs
DI Assistants. . . . . Dan Goslee
James Cody Baker
VP Feature Sales . . . . Jackie Lee
Visual Effects by. . . . . Encore Hollywood
VFX Producer . . . . Tom Kendall
CGI Artists . . . . Mitch Gates
Kurt McKeever
Changsoo Eun
Rodrigo Washington
Dan Lopez
Visual Effects by . . . . Ollin Studio
VFX Supervisor . . . . Charlie Iturriaga

Visual Effects by . . . . Riot
VFX Supervisor . . . . Jamie Hallett
Executive Producer . . . . Lindsay Burnett
VFX Producer. . . . . Erika McKee
VFX Coordinator . . . . Tony Barger
Digital Asset Manager . . . . . Mark Edwards
Assistant Digital Asset Manager . . . Dustin Foster
VFX Production Assistant. . . . . . Marla Neto
CG Supervisor . . . . Andrew Wilkoff
FX. . . . . Hiroyuki Okubo
Tracking & Integration Lead . . . . Tim Conway
Compositor . . . . Shane Wicklund
Roto/Paint. . . . . Robert Tatum
Cecile F. Tecson
Roto/Dustbust . . . . Mai Suzuki

Music Recorded and Mixed by . . Jeffrey Biggers
Additional Recording by . . . . . . Lars Stalfors
Soloists . . . . Lorne Balfe
Lili Hayden
Atli Örvarsson
Satnam Ramgotra
Music Editor . . . . Joanie Diener
Technical Score Engineers. . . Thomas Broderick
Peter "Oso" Snell
Assistant Engineer . . . . Katia Lewin
Score Recorded and Mixed at. . Remote Control
Productions, Santa Monica, CA
Music Productions Services . . . . Steven Kofsky
Music Production Coordinator . . . Andrew Zack
Studio Manager for
Remote Control Productions. . . Czarina Russell
Source Music Coordinator . . . . Libby Umstead

SONGS
"Falling Star"
Written by Ali Theodore, Henry Hey, Alana da
Fonseca, Zach Denziger
Performed by E Wilson
Courtesy of DeeTown Entertainment

"No More"
Written by Toots Camarata, Bob Russell
Performed by Madeleine Peyroux
Courtesy of Rounder Records
By arrangement with Ocean Park Music Group

"Mi Prietita Consentida"
Written by Ruben Ramos
Performed by Ruben Ramos and The Mexican
Revolution
Courtesy of Revolution Records
Under license from/by arrangement with
Jua Mos License and Publishing

"Transcontinental 1:30AM"
Written by Vienna Teng
Performed by Vienna Teng
Courtesy of Rounder Records
By arrangement with Ocean Park Music Group

"Las Golondrinas"
Written by Ricardo Palmerin & Luis Rosado
Performed by Flaco Jimenez
Courtesy of Warner Bros. Records Inc.
By arrangement with Warner Music Group
Film & TV Licensing

"Dewberry Wine"
Written by Julianna Raye
Performed by Julianna Raye
Courtesy of Chrysalis Music Group

"Quiero Verte"
Written by Martin T. Martinez (Roland Garcia
Music / BMI)
Performed by Mando Lopez Y Los Muchachos
Under license from: Hacienda Records

2929 Senior Vice President of Production
. . . . Mike Upton
Assistant to Mr. Upton . . . . . . Kandis Erickson
2929 Physical Production
. . . . Dorottya Hegedus-Lum
Assistants to Mr. Wuertemburg . . . Trevor Byrne
Sam Molleur
Production Counsel . . . . . . Sheppard Mullin
2929 Business Affairs . . . . Jessica Roddy
Heather Wayland
Chris Matson
Assistant to Business Affairs . . . Ellen Nicholson
Immigration Legal Services Provided by
. . . . Jim Saunders
Ralph Ehrenpreis
Insurance Provided by . . Gallagher Entertainment
A division of Arthur J. Gallagher
Risk Managment Services
Completion Guaranty Provided by
. . . . International Film Guarantors
Payroll Services Provided by
. . . . Entertainment Partners
Production Film & Video Dailies . . . . . Deluxe
Dolby Sound Consultant . . . . Bryan Pennington
Film Color Timer . . . . Kenny Becker
Cameras Provided by . . . . Panavision
Lighting Supplied by . . . . Paskal Lighting
Grip Equipment Supplied by
. . . . Grip Jet Equipment

Camera Dollies, Camera Car & Remote Camera
Systems by
. . . . Chapman/Leonard Studio Equipment, Inc.
Avids Provided by . . . . Pivotal Post
Titles by . . . . Pacific Title
Rights/Clearances by
. . . . Entertainment Clearances, Inc.
Cassandra Barbour
Laura Sevier
Product Placement Company
. . . . Stone Management
Product Placement Coordinators . . . Adam Stone
Cat Stone
"Coach" Clip courtesy of Universal Studios
Licensing LLLP

Filmed in part on location in
New Mexico
Support and Contribution by
Oregon Production Investment Fund
Administered by the
Oregon Economic and Community Development
Department
and by the Oregon Film & Video Office

The Film Makers Wish to Thank
New Mexico Film Office
Creative Media Institute for Film & Digital Arts,
NMSU
Department of Animal and Range Sciences,
NMSU
The City of Portland
Boost Mobile
Classic Images
KPTV
Kmart
Schwinn
Rolling Stone Magazine
Thought Equity Motion
Carlos Arriaga Alarid
Amelia Jordán de Arriaga
Carlos Arriaga Jordán
Patricia Arriaga Jordán
Jorge Arriaga Jordán
Lorenzo Vigas
Patricio Saíz
Simón Bross
Shana Eddy
Keya Khayatian
Linda Lichter
Michael Fitzgerald
Santiago Aguirre
Nick Clainos
Jimena Rodríguez

Manuel Tron
Gabriel Ripstein
Lourdes Revora
Luis Morales
Lucas Akoskin
Octavio García Allende
Lorena Pérez Jácome
Fernando Llanos
Dan Carrillo
Jesus Rodriguez
Johanna Morales
Ignacio Armendariz
Rosa Maria Lopez de Armendariz
Jonathan Benson
John Boren, PhD
Eduardo Costantini
Alex Garcia
Mark Medoff

ABOUT THE WRITER/DIRECTOR

Writer-director Guillermo Arriaga is one of today's most original story-telling voices and makes his directorial debut with *The Burning Plain*. As a screenwriter and now a director, Arriaga spins exhilaratingly complex, emotional, and provocative tapestries of human lives under intense pressure. His acclaimed and award-winning films—which include *Babel*, *21 Grams*, *Amores Perros*, and *The Three Burials of Melquiades Estrada*, the latter of which won the Best Screenplay Award at the Cannes Film Festival in 2005—traverse a dazzling range of subject matters, characters and moods, yet share in common a visceral, often luminous, portrait of humanity.

For his insightful, thought-provoking work on *Babel*, Arriaga received numerous honors, including an Academy Award® nomination for Best Original Screenplay and nominations from the Writers Guild of America, BAFTA, and the Hollywood Foreign Press Association. The film garnered a total of seven Academy Award® nominations, including Best Picture and was named among the 10 best of the year by more than groups and publications, including The National Board of Review, American Film Institute, *The New York Times, Rolling Stone,* and received the Golden Globe Award for Best Dramatic Film of 2006.

Shot in three continents and in five languages, *Babel* explores with shattering realism the nature of the barriers that separate mankind. The film encompasses many of the resonant themes that Arriaga has continued to explore for the last twenty-five years: the challenges of communication, the importance of love, the consequences of our actions, the contradictions of human nature, the clashes between differing cultural points of view, and the enigma of contemporary isolation, both physical and emotional.

Born and raised in Mexico City, and educated at the Ibero-American University, Arriaga first came to the fore in Mexico as a novelist. His works, rife with a trademark sense of humor and irony, include *Guillotine Squad* (1991), *A Sweet Smell of Death* (1994), and *The Night Buffalo* (1999), as well as a book of short stories, *Retorno 201* (2003), written when he was just twenty-four. They have been translated in eighteen languages and Arriaga has been cited by several critics as being among the most influential writers of our time.

In 1985, Arriaga suffered a serious car accident, which he later used as the basis for the film trilogy that began with *Amores Perros*, the first of three collaborations with director Alejandro González Iñárritu. Starring Gabriel Garcia Bernal and Adriana Barraza, the film explores the radiating effects of a single automobile crash on its various participants: the injured, the guilty, and the witness.

The success of the film brought Arriaga his first taste of the global reach of cinema. After winning over international critics who hailed *Amores Perros* as an instant cinematic classic, the film received an Oscar® nomination for Best Foreign Language Film, and won the BAFTA Award in the same category in 2001. It would also soon become regarded as one of the first Mexican films to cross over into the Hollywood spotlight, presaging a new generation of filmmakers who have energized international moviemaking.

Amores Perros also introduced Arriaga's fresh, invigorating style of piecing together emotionally gripping stories as intricate, interlocking human puzzles. With this film, Arriaga announced his ambitious intention, followed ever since, to explore screenplays as literary creations, using the same care for language, structure, and character development as any novel. Academics and critics who have followed his work have seen a close interplay of themes, vital concerns, and structures between his novels and his screenplays.

Arriaga's on-screen exploration of the nature of fate and coincidence continued with the second film of the trilogy with González Iñárritu: *21 Grams*, starring Sean Penn, Naomi Watts and Benicio Del Toro, a film on which he also served as associate producer. Arriaga received a BAFTA nomination for his screenplay, and the film received Oscar® nominations for Watts and Del Toro, and was included on many year-end "Best Of"

lists in 2003. Arriaga constructed the three intertwining stories of *21 Grams* around a freak accident which sets in motion an intricate emotional web among a group of intriguingly disparate characters: a critically ill mathematician, a grieving mother, and a born-again ex-con. Arriaga's contributions to the film were further celebrated that year by the Independent Spirit Awards which gave *21 Grams* its Special Distinction Award.

Before completing the trilogy about the consequences of modern life, Arriaga took a detour. He next embarked on a piercing yet poetic journey into justice, loyalty, and friendship with his screenplay for *The Three Burials of Melquiades Estrada*, directed by and starring Tommy Lee Jones in the story of a man who sets out to bury his friend in his Mexican hometown. Arriaga won the prestigious Best Screenplay Award at the Cannes Film Festival in 2005. A wholly unexpected take on the American Western, *The Three Burials of Melquiades Estrada* further demonstrated Arriaga's capacity to develop spellbinding stories in vastly different genres yet rife with his very personal themes.

In addition to his feature films and novels, Arriaga has also directed, produced and written short films, documentaries, television series, radio and television commercials, and has been a college professor for more than twenty-five years.